The Caledonian Companion

by

Alastair J. Hardie

THE CALEDONIAN COMPANION

'The new Bible for fiddlers'
KENNETH KEMP, *Aberdeen Evening Express*

'A valuable addition to any fiddle-player's bookshelf.'

The Scots Magazine

'It must rank among the most attractive publications of its kind, in a word a classic.'
LEONARD FRIEDMAN, *What's On*

'Both beginners and practised violinists— even practising Scottish fiddlers—can find a lot of enjoyment and learn a lot in *The Caledonian Companion.*'
ALAN BRUFORD, *The Broadsheet*

'An indispensable addition to fiddle lore . . . *The Caledonian Companion* offers the best of all written fiddle worlds.'
ALASTAIR CLARK, *The Scotsman*

'Here, for the first time, the techniques of Scots fiddling are thoroughly analysed and presented in a progressive, logical order which makes them easy to grasp. . . . The book's scholarly aspects are also handled in exemplary fashion . . . No Scots fiddle tutor remotely like this has been written before.'

DAVID JOHNSON,
Times Educational Supplement

The Caledonian Companion

*A Collection of Scottish Fiddle Music
and Guide to its Performance*

by

Alastair J. Hardie

The Hardie Press

The publisher acknowledges subsidy from the
Scottish **A**rts Council
towards the publication of this volume

ISBN 0 946868 08 5

Originally published in 1981 by EMI Music Publishing Ltd.

This edition published in Great Britain 1992 by The Hardie Press,
17 Harrison Gardens, Edinburgh, EH11 1SE

Second Impression 1995
Third Impression 2003

Printed in Great Britain by Hobbs the Printers, Totton, Hampshire

Selected items from this publication are available on an associated recording
The Fiddler's Companion (HPCD001) produced under licence from EMI Records UK, Ltd.

ACKNOWLEDGEMENTS

I would like to record my thanks to Tom Anderson and Bill Hardie for permission to quote original compositions and for sets as played by these two artists; to Aly Bain and Angus Grant for the tunes in their settings; to James F. Dickie for some slow strathspey variations; to Seamus MacNeill for enabling me to reproduce a composition by Archibald MacNeill.

I am indebted to the Henderson sisters (Esther, Jeannie and Mary) for permission to quote from J. Murdoch Henderson's *Flowers of Scottish Melody* and *Scottish Music Maker* and to Messrs. Bayley & Ferguson Ltd. for enabling the re-printing of *Back to the Hills, Buckingham House, Macpherson's Lament* and *The Devil and the Dirk*.

The research process (gathering of facts, dates, documentation, manuscripts etc.) was greatly aided by Mary Anne Alburger, Alan Bruford and Peter Cooke (both of The School of Scottish Studies, Edinburgh University), James and Ivory Duncan, Dr. David Johnson, Mrs. Ethel Key, Mrs. Elsie MacAndrew, Captain John MacLellan and the music staff of The National Library of Scotland. The three tunes ''as played by Angus Grant'' were transcribed from recorded perform-ances with the assistance of Veronique Nelson. My thanks go to all these people.

A special debt of gratitude is accorded to Bill Hardie for his collaboration in the bowing of the tunes. His support has been a constant inspiration.

A.J.H., 1981

FOREWORD TO THE NEW EDITION

Ten years have elapsed since this volume first appeared in print. It may be of interest to the reader to know what significant alterations and additions the book has undergone since its initial publication.

The 1986 reprint added an appendix index and corrected the errors and oversights a first edition is inevitably heir to; these included the addition of bowings for *Mrs. Janet B. Hardie* and *The Dean Brig o'Edinburgh*. A small bowing alteration at the end of *The Liverpool Hornpipe* came more into the category of a change in the light of experience, a description which might also apply to the new bowing now undertaken in *The Duchess Tree* and the re-thought illustration relating to the trill (page 105, ex. 43).

The death of such personalities as Tom Anderson, James F. Dickie and Robert Innes has necessitated the emendation of the entries pertaining to these men. I have also completed the biography of my late father and partner at The Hardie Press, William (Bill) Hardie.

Which brings me to the most ostensible and significant change—that of the publisher. With the reappearance of *The Caledonian Companion* from The Hardie Press, the prodigal has indeed returned—not only to the family but also to the country of origin.

ALASTAIR J. HARDIE
EDINBURGH
NOVEMBER 1991 & 1995

CONTENTS

This book is dedicated to the *Fiddling Hardies*: **Matthew Hardie, Thomas Hardie, Peter Hardie, William Hardie, Charles Hardie, James Hardie, William Hardie (jnr.)** and **Bill Hardie**, whose contributions as fiddle makers, players and composers have so notably enriched Scottish musical life during the past 200 years.

Nae cotillion, brent new frae France
But hornpipes, jigs, strathspeys, and reels,
Put life and mettle in their heels.

Robert Burns

The Hardies

The art of music-making has often produced particular families whose involvement has extended down through several generations, the skills being handed on from father to son. Scottish traditional fiddling has proved no exception in this respect with such famous names as the Allan family from Forfar, the Cummings from Speyside and the Gows from Dunkeld.

No family, however, can claim such an unbroken, wide ranging and dedicated commitment to the cause of Scottish fiddling than the Hardie family. In the realms of both performance and violin-making, the Hardies' contribution has been unique and could easily justify a complete book. The following lines summarize the principal figures, their biographical details and achievements.

Chronologically, the story begins with **Matthew Hardie** who was born in Edinburgh in 1755. The probability is that he trained as a cabinet-maker and studied the art of violin-making with a certain John Blair. Hardie established a flourishing violin-making and repair business in the Low Calton area of his native city, finding sufficient time to pass on his skills to the younger generation of Scottish violin-makers including Thomas Hardie (his son) and Peter Hardie (his full cousin).

Eventually the importation of cheap German factory-made fiddles seriously affected the business, and the latter stages of his career were clouded by confinement in the debtor's jail. He died in St. Cuthbert's Poorhouse on the 30th of August, 1826 and was buried in Edinburgh's Greyfriars' Churchyard.

Hardie generally followed the Amati and Stradivari models, remaining faithful to the originals in respect of body length, width of bouts, depth of ribs and height of arching. He used a spirit varnish which ranged in colour from pale amber to yellow-brown or yellow-red but which has now mostly dulled to a brownish colour.

Commenting on Hardie's work in his *Scottish Violin Makers: Past and Present* (1910), William C. Honeyman writes:

It is evident that the graceful lines of his violins and the perfect contour of his scrolls have come intuitively from the man's brain more than from his patterns. . . . in every one of his violins there is apparent in every line that subtle *something* which no one can define but which is seen as clearly in the roughest work of Joseph Guarneri (del Jesu). It is the same with the tone. The trained ear at once notes that it is not a commonplace tone, though it sometimes takes a firm hand to show its real grandeur.

With such critical acclaim, it is not surprising then that Matthew Hardie has come to be regarded as the doyen of Scottish violin makers. The following is an example of one of Hardie's labels printed in type on white paper, the last two figures being handwritten:

Matthew's son **Thomas Hardie** was born in Edinburgh circa 1804. His apprenticeship in violin-making began around the surprisingly early age of ten and continued for twelve years until his father's death in 1826. Thomas carried on the business from his father's old shop, but later moved to successive premises in Shakespeare Square (beside the North Bridge) and the High Street. His final move was to the Lawnmarket and it was there on the 19th of January, 1858 that he died tragically as a result of falling down stairs. He is buried beside his father in Greyfriars' Churchyard.

Thomas Hardie's work is characterised by craftsmanship of a high order; the varnish, beautifully applied, is of a yellowish-pale red colour. Despite his adoption of the same Amati and Stradivari models as Matthew Hardie, his instruments cannot be favourably compared tonally with his father's best work.

Although occasionally handwritten, his labels were usually printed in type on white paper e.g.: THOMAS HARDIE, Fecit., Edinburgh, Anno 1846

Peter Hardie, the son of an army surgeon, was born (probably abroad) circa 1775, but spent most of his life in the Dunkeld area of Perthshire. Generally known as "Highland Hardie" he was a man of imposing appearance and powerful physique. He died in November, 1863 and was buried in Dowally Churchyard, seven miles above Dunkeld.

Hardie was a favourite pupil of the famous Niel Gow and became a skilled executant and composer in the traditional style. While studying at Edinburgh University he was a frequent visitor to the workshop of his cousin Matthew Hardie and it was from this master that he learned the craft of violin-making. In turn, Peter Hardie, passed on his expertise to Willie Blair of Aberdeenshire, the so-called Queen's Fiddler, and to his grandson James Hardie.

His model is a cross between that of Stainer and Amati. "The Scroll", according to Wm. C. Honeyman, "is turned sharply out at the edges in the style of Joseph Ruddiman, whose violins Hardie had probably seen and admired. The violins are all neatly purfled, and the tone is usually large and mellow."

He usually identified his instruments by stamping his name on the back below the button: **P. HARDIE**.

It was with Peter Hardie's son **William Hardie** (1787 - 1884) that the family moved (around 1830) from Perthshire to Aberdeenshire in the north-east of Scotland. The move initially was to Sauchen Tree near the village of Methlick, and subsequently (c. 1835) to Aquhadley, near Ellon. The family finally put down roots in the Methlick area where Hardie became a tenant of the croft of "Auchencruive".

William Hardie married Mary Strachan (1805 - 1910) the daughter of another celebrated north-east fiddler John Strachan "Drumnagarrow". They had a family of no fewer than fifteen, several of whom were subsequently to distinguish themselves musically. William himself, like his father before him, combined the talents of composer and player, although he was probably more of a specialist on the 'cello than the *sma' fiddle*.

In his latter years — he was 97 years of age when he died — *auld Willie* took to wandering off down the main road; one of the sons would retrieve the old man and on being questioned where he was making for Willie would invariably reply that he was going back home to Perthshire. The experiences of youth and the nostalgia for the Gow country obviously exerted a magnetic power which even old-age could not dim.

James Hardie, son of William Hardie, was born at Aquhadley on the 1st of January, 1836. At the tender age of nine the young James received his first lessons in violin-making from his grand-father, Peter Hardie. He went on to make his first complete instrument when he was fifteen years old and eventually set up business in Edinburgh where, in a long career, he produced over two thousand instruments. He died in 1916 at the age of eighty.

Although he also worked to Guarneri and Stradivari models, his best instruments were undoubtedly those based on Maggini. These are often characterised by use of double purfling and ornamentation on the back. His varnish has a fossil-amber base and is of a golden amber or golden red colour. Hardie's talents as a luthier were complemented by considerable practical skill as a player of strathspeys and reels.

James Hardie's work has received considerable critical acclaim. In his *British Violin Makers* (1904), W. Meredith Morris refers to instruments "which for excellence of material, workmanship and tone are unsurpassed" and Wm C. Honeyman rated him amongst the finest contemporary Scottish makers.

The labels from his mature years are printed on white paper with obverse and reverse gold medals at each end.

Born at Aquhadley, **Charles Hardie** (1849 - 1893) was the son of William Hardie and brother of James. A carpenter by trade in the city of Aberdeen, he was considered "one of the best violinists in Scotland in his day". J. Scott Skinner was of the opinion that he excelled in slow airs, light reels and hornpipes, particularly "Banks". But this most exacting of critics goes further in his approbation and writing in the *Elgin Collection* states, "The composer considers that Mr. Charles Hardie, Aberdeen, is the finest exponent of his compositions living."

Charles Hardie's talents were accorded the official recognition of his being invited to play for Queen Victoria at Balmoral Castle. On being informed of his untimely death at the age of 44 the Queen is said to have expressed her own personal feeling of loss at the passing of this talented musician.

William Hardie Jnr. (c. 1856 - 1944), son of William Hardie and brother of James and Charles, was born at "Auchencruive". A good exponent of the slow strathspey, dance strathspey and reel, he was a man whose talents, far in advance of the average country fiddler, were much in demand at local dances and functions. His musical friends included J.F. Dickie of New Deer and William Duguid, Fyvie.

Following the death of his youngest child Annie — she was struck down with meningitis at the age of 9 — he was so grief-stricken that he gave up the fiddle for a period of some twenty years. Time however is a great healer and he eventually returned to his music, continuing to play right up to his death in his 88th year.

Grandson of William Hardie Jnr. and son of John Hardie, an Aberdeen engineer, **Bill Hardie** was born in Aberdeen in 1916. His enthusiasm for the fiddle was first kindled by the playing of his grandfather at "Auchencruive" and this, together with the playing of J.F. Dickie and the recordings of J. Scott Skinner, can be cited as his principal influences. This was combined with a sound conventional training from two respected Aberdeen teachers, Theodore Crozier and Alex. Smith.

Bill Hardie achieved competitive success at Aberdeen in 1937 by winning a challenge cup for the performance of J. Scott Skinner's strathspey and reel compositions. Again in 1951 he won the slow air and march, strathspey and reel classes at the Banchory and Mintlaw festivals.

Other significant activities included innumerable broadcasts for the B.B.C., (the first undertaken at the age of sixteen), recording, adjudication, teaching and, from 1965-67, the conductorship of the Aberdeen Strathspey and Reel Society. Of particular interest was his lifelong friendship with J. Murdoch Henderson (1902-1972), whose *Scottish Music Maker* (1957) testifies to a highly fruitful collaboration between collector and player. He appeared in print in his own right with *The Beauties of the North* (1986) a collection of fifty melodies in unique settings.

The historic links with Methlick continued until 1981 for, up till his retirement from Grampian Regional Education Committee, Bill Hardie taught the violin at the local village school, where so many of his forebears were educated. On moving to Edinburgh in 1986, Bill joined in partnership with his son Alastair Hardie (the author of the present volume) in a music publishing business—The Hardie Press. He made an inestimable contribution to this right up to his death in 1995.

The picture emerges then of a family's emotional and professional involvement throughout a wide range of the art and craft of music. The work of these men and the tradition which they represent has been sustained by convictions of social usefulness and artistic value. Their achievement has a relevance both for our awareness of the past and as an inspiration to how our culture can survive the present day curse of pre-packaged, faceless conformity.

The Hardies — A Family Album

Matthew Hardie (1755-1826)
The Scottish Stradivari

Peter Hardie (c1775-1863)
Highland Hardie

John Strachan "Drumnagarrow"
Celebrated fiddler

James Hardie (1836-1916)
Fiddle maker — inherited the
mantle of Matthew Hardie

Charles Hardie (1849-1893)
The Methlick Wonder

William Hardie Jnr. (c1856-1944)
His playing preserved a family
tradition

Bill Hardie (1916-1995)
Celebrated exponent of the
Scott Skinner style

The drawings of Matthew, Peter and James Hardie are taken from *Scottish Violin Makers —
past and present* (1910) by William C. Honeyman.

Photographs of John Strachan, Charles and William Hardie by courtesy of Mr and Mrs Angus
Shaw and Mr and Mrs W. H. Jaffray.

Major Fiddle Composers

"The Father of Strathspey and Reel Players"

"The Greatest Preserver and Improver of the Age"

Niel Gow (1727-1807)
(Scottish National Portrait Gallery)

Nathaniel Gow (1763-1831)
(National Library of Scotland)

Niel Gow, the son of a plaid-weaver, was born in the Perthshire village of Inver. He started playing the fiddle at the age of 9 and was largely self-taught. Apart from his characterful playing and his compositions (it is estimated he wrote around seventy tunes), Gow's influence on Scottish music continued through the activities of his four sons, Andrew, John, William and Nathaniel, all of whom were practising musicians.

It was Niel's youngest son Nathaniel Gow who most generously inherited his father's genius. Apart from being a notable fiddler and teacher, Nathaniel was a gifted composer and founder (in 1796) of a music publishing business in Edinburgh.

Of the Gow publications, the first four *Collections of Strathspey Reels* (1784, 1788, 1792 and 1800) were the work of "Niel Gow at Dunkeld". The fifth and sixth collections (1809 and 1822) and the four *Repositories* (1799, 1802, 1806 and 1817), on the other hand, were by "Niel Gow and Sons".

After their meeting in 1787, Robert Burns left the following memorable description of the legendary Perthshire fiddler:

A short, stout-built honest Highland figure, with his greyish hair shed on his honest social brow.

17

William Marshall (1748-1833)
(Scottish National Portrait Gallery)

Marshall was born at Fochabers in Morayshire. At the age of twelve, after an education lasting a brief six months, he entered the service of the Duke of Gordon, a position in which he spent his entire working life. The duties of house-steward however were sufficiently undemanding to leave ample time for him to develop his abilities as architect, astronomer, clock-maker, mathematician and above all fiddler/composer.

Marshall's 287 tunes were presented in three collections:

A Collection of Strathspey Reels (1781)
Scottish Airs, Melodies, Strathspeys and Reels (1822)
Scottish Melodies, Reels, Strathspeys (posthumously published in 1847)

The following lines from the introduction to the 1847 Collection leave no doubt as to Marshall's executive talents:

> His style was characterised by fullness of intonation, precision and brilliancy of expression . . . .
> and so inspiring was the effect, that when he played reels or strathspeys, the inclination to
> dance on the part of old and young became irresistible.

Simon Fraser (1773-1852)
(National Library of Scotland)

Fraser was born at Ardachie near Fort Augustus and later moved to Stratherrick, where he became the tenant of "Knockie". This is the name sometimes given to his great collection, *The Airs and Melodies peculiar to the Highlands of Scotland and the Isles* (1816). This work, full of the nostalgia of the 1715-45 Jacobite period, contains 230 tunes, the majority of which were collected by his grandfather and father, John.

A small extract from a second volume was published in Inverness in 1874. The rest of the book, prepared by Fraser's son Angus, exists only in manuscript.

James Scott Skinner (1843-1927)

Skinner was born in the Kincardineshire town of Banchory. His brother Sandy gave him his first fiddle lessons and taught him the art of vamping on the 'cello. It was as an accompanist in this capacity that Skinner first met Peter Milne, "The Tarland Minstrel", and it was from this source that he learned the art of strathspey-playing.

The more formal side of his musical education began in 1855 when he embarked on a six-year apprenticeship as a member of *Dr. Mark's Little Men*, a celebrated juvenile orchestra of the day. During this time he also had lessons from Charles Rougier, a violinist with the Hallé orchestra.

Apart from his busy concert and recording career, Skinner found time to compose some 600 tunes, most of which are to be found in his five major published collections:

Miller o' Hirn Collection (1881)
Elgin Collection (1884)
Logie Collection (1888)
The Scottish Violinist (1900)
Harp and Claymore Collection (1904).

An example of James Scott Skinners' manuscript

The widespread feeling of loss, following Skinner's death in 1927, is poignantly caught in the following lines by George Riddell:

Nae langer Skinner's fiddle rings
Cauld now the haund that touched the strings
The thocht o't still a saut tear brings
    To mony an e'e.
For king was he 'mang a' the kings
    O' minstrelsy.

John Murdoch Henderson (1902-1972)
(By Courtesy of the Henderson Family)

Henderson was born at Oldwhat, New Deer, Aberdeenshire, and educated at Peterhead Academy and Aberdeen University. A schoolmaster by profession, he published two collections, *The Flowers of Scottish Melody* (1935), an anthology which included some of his own compositions, and *The Scottish Music Maker* (1957), an edition of the music of J. Scott Skinner. With his unrivalled historical knowledge and his very real talent as a composer, Henderson emerges as one of the most creative figures in Scottish traditional music in the 20th century.

Forms in Traditional Music

Hornpipe

The hornpipe was a primitive double-reed wind instrument dating from around the 13th century. The dance and its related music came to have its maritime associations around the middle of the 18th century. As many ships' companies carried a resident fiddler, music was readily available for dancing, thus providing a much needed form of daily exercise.

Much of the even-rhythmed passage-work co-incides with the style of the reel, but the dotted rhythms, characteristic of so many hornpipes, were a later mid-19th century innovation. There is a marked differentiation in tempo between even and uneven-rhythmed hornpipes:— the former are generally played at ♩ = 104 - 112, whereas the latter tend to the more relaxed ♩ = 69 - 76.

Jig

Giga, *Gigue* and *Geige* are all titles for the "fidil", the modern violin's ancestor of twelve to fifteen hundred years ago. The jig probably derives its name from the sort of music played on these instruments. Although mainly associated with the music of Ireland, the jig occupies an honourable place in Scottish traditional music. It is cast in compound time, either duple ($\frac{6}{8}$) or triple ($\frac{9}{8}$) and can be played from a moderate tempo of ♩. = 116 - 120 to a sprightly tempo of ♩. = 126 - 138.

Lament

Usually cast in the pastoral or slow air genre, this is a composition to commemorate a person's death.

March

Imbued with the spirit of the Scottish fighting man, the march is normally written in common time and played at a tempo of ♩ = 92 - 100. Playing pipe marches on the fiddle is an important part of the repertoire and these are written in $\frac{2}{4}$ or $\frac{6}{8}$ time.

Pastoral

Like the slow air and slow strathspey, this is music for listening to and was not designed for dance purposes. Played in a slow or moderate tempo (♩ = 52 - 56), this was a form particularly cultivated by J. Scott Skinner.

Polka

Originating in Bohemia around the 1830's, the polka is usually written in $\frac{2}{4}$ time and played at a tempo of ♩ = 76 - 84. It is often associated with display-music of a rather virtuoso nature.

Rant

The word is of Germanic origin meaning to *frolic* or *romp* and denotes a lively reel or strathspey-type tune often characterised by a use of the rhythm ♫♩ Many tunes, familiar today as *strathspeys*, appeared originally as *rants*. The tempo is similar to that of the strathspey, i.e., ♩ = 132 - 138.

Reel

This is a form common to Scotland, Ireland and England and today implies a sprightly, even-rhythmed tune in fast tempo. Many of the reels in J. Scott Skinner's *The Scottish Violinist* are marked to be played at ♩ = 136 and in our own day Aly Bain and Bill Hardie will take such pieces as *Mrs. Forbes Leith* and *Speed the Plough* in the region of ♩ = 120 - 128. Most reels, however, will benefit from the less breathless tempo of ♩ = c. 108 - 116.

As to the style of reel-playing, one can do no better than quote Skinner's words from *A Guide to Bowing*:—

"The reel should be played crisp and birly like a weel-gaun wheelie."

Schottische

A strathspey-like tune accented in a way which implies more of a ${2 \atop 2}$ metre than the strathspey's common time; correspondingly the tempo can be rather faster than that of the average strathspey.

Scots Measure

This made its first appearance in print around 1700. It is distinguished by a use of *anacrusis* and a stressing of the first three quavers of the bar and tempi which can vary from a leisurely ♩ = 100 - 108 to a lively ♩ = c. 120. The rhythmic structure of the *Scots measure* often hints at the hornpipe of over a century later.

Slow Air

A form of solo-music giving the player a chance to display beauty of tone and phrase at a relaxed tempo (♩ = c. 56).

Slow Strathspey

Here the form, rhythms and bowing technique of the dance-strathspey is applied to music of a slower tempo (♩ = 60 - 69). By traditional standards, the choice of keys is often more adventurous, Bb and Eb being particular favourites. Skinner applied the title "solo strathspey" to this form.

Song Air

These compositions, usually of the slow air genre, were once the melodies of songs and wedded to a text.

Strathspey

The earliest examples of this form emerged around 1749 and were known as "strathspey reels". Its structure hinges upon the rhythms ♫ and ♫. and undoubtedly provides our music's greatest challenge to bowing-technique. The dance-strathspey, moulded from the character of the fiddle itself, has developed into the most important form of Scottish traditional music. The tempo can vary from ♩ = 126 to ♩ = 138.

Introduction

Nature of the Book

The Caledonian Companion has a three-fold function. First it is a collection of Scottish traditional fiddle music, most of which is not currently available, a significant portion being published for the first time. Secondly it is a fiddle tutor, *i.e.*, it sets out to elucidate a range of techniques which are essential for the idiomatic rendition of traditional music. And thirdly it provides a pocket history to each tune: information on the composer (if known), the source collection, the set used, explanations of the many colourful and unusual titles and relevant background detail to the historical and contemporary fiddle scene.

Sources of the Tunes

The major source for the tunes is the great collections of fiddle music which were published mainly between the years 1700 - 1935. The principal composers/collectors featured are Niel and Nathaniel Gow, William Marshall, Simon Fraser, J. Scott Skinner and J. Murdoch Henderson.

Although original sources have, where possible, been consulted, the tunes are mostly presented in sets which conform to the traditional playing-styles of the present day. The description "as played by", will frequently be found throughout the book, emphasising the importance of the performer's contribution to the realisation of this music.

Fiddle Tutor

"Of course there were natural geniuses, such as the immortals:— Captain Simon Fraser, Niel Gow, Marshall, Red Rob, Duncan Macintyre, Airchie Menzies, Peter Milne, Drumnagarrow (John Strachan), Geordie Donald, James Young, Alexander Skinner, Charles Hardie. All these men did good work, but would have soared even higher had they received a good sound training in manual equipment, and still remembered to render their country's music by the light of nature, maintaining its ruggedness and character, and not making it insipid and genteel."

If justification were required for the fiddle-tutor aspect of this collection, then it is provided in the above quotation from J. Scott Skinner's *A Guide to Bowing* (c1900). Indeed, honourable mention must be made of this short treatise which, together with the *Gillespie Manuscript* (1768) (an unpublished fiddle tutor by James Gillespie of Perth) and *The Strathspey, Reel and Hornpipe Tutor for the Violin* (1898) by William Honeyman, constitutes the principal achievements of the past in teaching the arts of Scottish traditional fiddling.

The author is hopeful that *The Caledonian Companion* will represent a modern parallel to the distinguished work of these predecessors.

The tunes at the beginning assume a command of basic skills in playing and reading. Bowing, fingering and ornamentation peculiar to this music are then progressively introduced, equipping the player eventually with the technical know-how for tackling anything from *Tullochgoram* to *The President*. All the common major and minor keys are dealt with in turn and a system of fingering-charts has been included to introduce them.

As will be seen, all the tunes are fully bowed, representing one fiddler's particular interpretation. They are not to be regarded however as the final word and it is suggested that, having assimilated the considerable range of bowing techniques taught within these covers, players can then decide on their own interpretation.

Notation

For the most part, the practice has been adopted throughout the book, of writing reels and hornpipes in $\frac{2}{4}$ time. This is felt to give a better idea of pulse. The one significant exception to this involves the four Shetland tunes, *Da Auld Foula Reel*, *Da Grocer*, *Da Sixereen* and *Willa-fjord*. As prescribed by their composer/arranger, Tom Anderson, these are notated in *alla breve* time in the hope that this will have a moderating effect on the tempi chosen. As Tom said himself, ''Unfortunately Shetland reels are played much too fast today and would therefore be very difficult to dance to''.

Speed, Style and Dynamic Indications

In accordance with a tradition established by many great collections of the past, speed and style indications are, for the most part, given in English. Extensive variation in dynamics is stylistically more important in performance-music (pastorals, slow airs, slow strathspeys, sets of variations, violin solos, etc.) than it is in the music cast in dance tempo. This fact is reflected in the distribution of dynamic markings.

Tempi

Appropriate tempi are discussed in the section on "Forms in Traditional Music". When the tempo of a particular tune falls outside these recommended speeds, then specific metronome indications have been provided.

Performance Practice

Repetition   It can be assumed that most of the shorter pieces — hornpipes, jigs, strathspeys, reels, Scots measures, slow airs and pastorals, etc., — will be played twice; those pieces which have accompanying variations form an obvious exception to this rule.

When the process of repeating requires slight re-adjustments to the opening, this has been made clear in the text. A pause indication ($\frown$) placed above the final note of a piece is intended to apply only for the second time.

Abrupt Endings   A number of the strathspeys will appear to have abnormally abrupt endings (see for example *Tullochgorum* and *Buckingham House*). This can be explained by the fact that the strathspey is not usually treated as an entity in itself, being habitually followed by a reel or Scots measure. Because of the tutorial nature of this collection, it has not always been possible to follow a strathspey with a matching reel. To compensate for this, suggestions are given, whenever possible, for tunes which will form suitable groupings.

A large percentage of reels are notated with rather indeterminate endings and, as the reel will frequently conclude a group or set of tunes, it is important to find some satisfactory concluding formula. *The Deil amang the Tailors* (a), *Speed the Plough* (b) and *James Hardie* (c) typify the three most common problem endings. The conclusions illustrated below all employ triple-stopped chords. Depending on the key, however, it may be more appropriate to use double or quadruple-stopped chords.

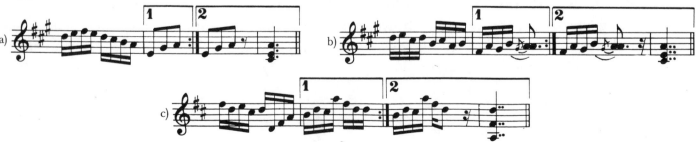

Accompaniment

All the material in this collection is presented for unaccompanied fiddle. It was the norm however, in the collections of the Gows, Fraser, Marshall and Skinner, to notate the tunes "with a bass", enabling them to be played with a vamp accompaniment on the 'cello, piano (harpsichord in the 18th century), harp or clarsach.

In our time some of the very greatest exponents of this music — Hector MacAndrew, Bill Hardie, Tom Anderson and J.F. Dickie — have invariably used some form of accompaniment, considering their performances denuded without such support.

Style

The subject of how a fiddle and bow should be held is a highly sensitive one. The spirit, as in so many aspects of fiddling, is more important than the letter: the great Niel Gow (as depicted in the celebrated Raeburn portrait on page 17) was hardly a proponent of the classically accepted style. It should be added however that the technically more demanding tunes in the book, with their use of the higher positions and a more advanced bowing technique, presuppose a conventional training.

To whom it may concern

The Caledonian Companion will appeal to the solo fiddler, the folk enthusiast, the *Strathspey and Reel Society* devotee and the classical violinist intent on broadening his horizons. It is hoped that this book will be of particular value to the younger generation, awakening new interest and enthusiasm in this vital, colourful music.

The Fiddler's Companion

A recording *The Fiddler's Companion* (HPCD001) has been produced in association with *The Caledonian Companion*. Including as it does, the playing of Alastair Hardie, Bill Hardie, Tom Anderson, Aly Bain, Angus Grant and Hector MacAndrew, this sets out to capture the magic of some of the most distinguished traditional players of our day.

Eighteen tunes from the album appear in *The Caledonian Companion* in the form of transcriptions of the recorded performance. Of these, fourteen are credited "as played by" the artist in question and the remaining four are original compositions by Tom Anderson, Alastair Hardie and Bill Hardie.

Valuable, and indeed essential, as these transcriptions are, it has never been the intention behind this project to freeze the music into stereotypes. To this end the record features a further twelve tunes which employ *The Caledonian Companion* text as a starting point for individual interpretation in respect of bowing, ornamentation, etc. A rare opportunity is thus provided of observing the traditional musician creating his art from the bare bones of the printed page.

The music from the concluding two tracks of the recording does not appear in this book. They feature the playing of Hector MacAndrew and were included as a memorial tribute to that great traditional violinist on his death in April, 1980.

The artist/tune track listings are as follows; the "as played by" items mentioned above are indicated by an asterisk (tune 1, track 11 is as played by Bill Hardie):

CHAPTER ONE

Scots Measures, Hornpipes and Reels

The White Cockade

Scots Measure
Moderately

This tune appeared in James Aird's Collection (Vol. I 1782) where it was known as *The Ranting Highlandman*. The white cockade was the symbol adopted by the followers of Prince Charles Edward Stuart in the 1745 Jacobite campaign.

The finger positions for the key of G major, in which this tune is written, are indicated on the chart opposite.

a) The sign V indicates an up bow (from point to heel), the sign ⊓ a down bow (from heel to point).

b) The curved lines joining notes are called *slurs* — play these notes smoothly in one bow direction.

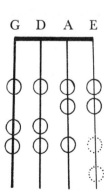

c) The use of the *straight slur* (as in bar 4) indicates that the notes are to be played in a staccato manner by a momentary stopping of the bow.

Ex. 1

written   played

There was a Lad was born in Kyle

Scots Measure

Moderately

A set of this appears in the *Gow Repository* (Part I, 1799) under the title *Watson's Scotch Measure*. It is now invariably associated with its present title since Robert Burns (1759 - 96) wedded it to his celebrated autobiographical lines.

a) The first 3 bars should be bowed in the following manner:

Ex. 2

upper half   point upper half   middle upper half   point

b) Bars 7, 8 and 16 employ a form of ornamentation known as the *Acciaccatura* (crushed note). This is played before the beat, with the accent falling on the note it embellishes:

Ex. 3

written   played

Much of the ornamentation in Scottish traditional fiddle music conforms to this pattern of being played *before* the beat. This is, of course, the opposite of the established practice in classical music. Nevertheless the signs used for such decorations are, for the most part, identical with those found in the more formal context.

The East Neuk o' Fife

Scots Measure
Lively

As played by A.J.H.

This tune was first published under its present title by William McGibbon (c.1690 - 1756), appearing in his 3rd Collection of 1755. This set is taken from J. Scott Skinner's *Harp and Claymore Collection* (1904).

    a) Keep the 1st finger down on the A-string for the duration of the line in bars 1-2 and 5-6.

    b) The second measure (or section) begins with an up-bow. This means that bars 9, 11 and 13-14 are *back-bowed*, (i.e., use an up-bow on the strong accent instead of the more customary down).

The Flowers of Edinburgh

Scots Measure
Lively

Variation by Bill Hardie

VARIATION

Described by J. Murdoch Henderson in the *Flowers of Scottish Melody* (1935) as "an air, unsurpassed by any other Scottish $\frac{2}{4}$ air in G of quick movement", this classic tune appeared in London in 1742 as a crude song entitled *My Love's bonny when she smiles on me*.

a) *Double-stopping* — the simultaneous performance of two notes, is featured in this tune. Finger the opening passage with a 3rd followed by a 2nd on the G string against an open D.

   Bar 12 of the variation features a form of double-stopping known as the *Unison*: the simultaneous sounding of two notes of the same pitch. The fingering is a 4th on the A against an open E.

b) *Fore-phrasing* is an important bowing-technique. Demonstrated here in the many across-the-bar slurrings, it recognises the primacy of the phrase as opposed to the bar line.

c) The "3" over the opening notes of the second measure (or section) in both the tune and variation indicates a *triplet*: a group of three notes played in the time of two of the same kind.

The North Shore

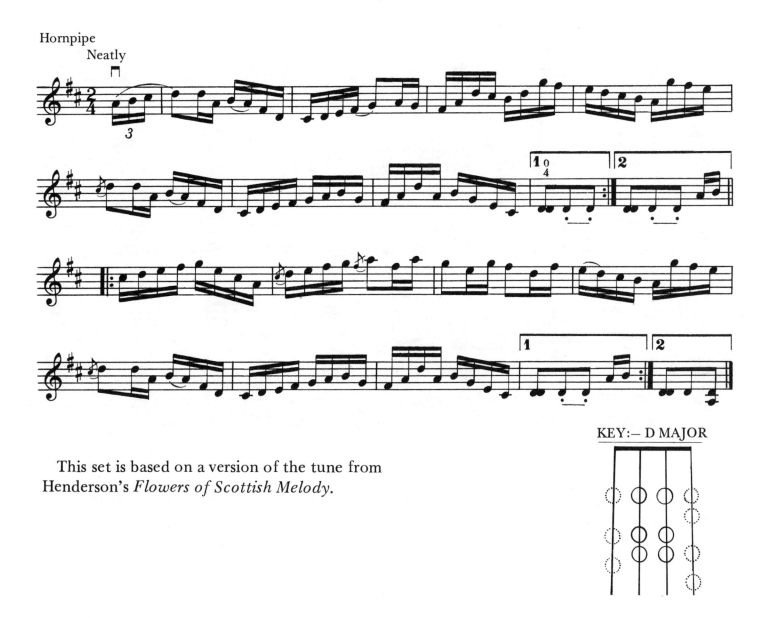

This set is based on a version of the tune from Henderson's *Flowers of Scottish Melody*.

KEY:— D MAJOR

The Liverpool Hornpipe

Hornpipe

As played by Bill Hardie

This tune appears in Vol. II of James Stewart Robertson's *Atholl Collection* (1884) and in Keith Norman MacDonald's *Skye Collection* (1887).

Willafjord

As played by Tom Anderson

Reel ♩= 102

This traditional Shetland reel came originally from Greenland, having been brought back at the end of the 19th century as a result of the Arctic whaling expeditions. It comes from a collection of Shetland fiddle-tunes entitled *Haand me doon da Fiddle* (1979) compiled by Tom Anderson and Pam Swing.

The characteristic *syncopations* (a displacing of the normal order of the stressed beats) in this tune are produced as a result of the *tied note* (notated with a curved line similar to the slur). This is a method of lengthening the duration of a sound by *tying* it to another of the same pitch. The opening of *Willafjord* could therefore be written:

Ex. 4  *etc.*

The Deil amang the Tailors

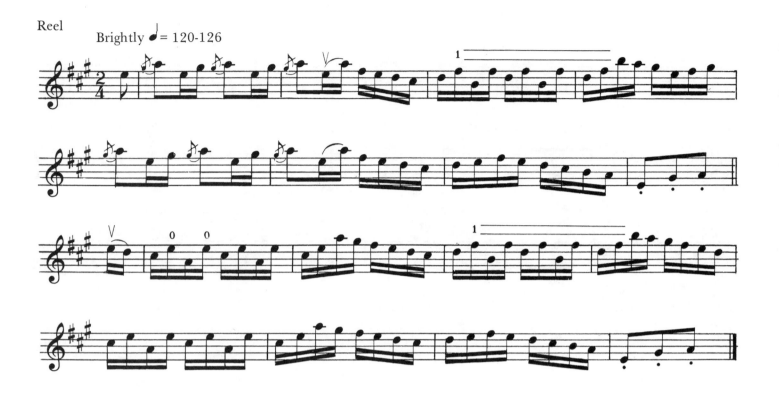

Reel

Brightly ♩ = 120-126

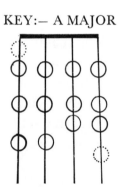

KEY:— A MAJOR

This celebrated tune appears in the *Atholl Collection*.

a) The sign 1══ over bars 3-4 and 11-12 indicates that the 1st finger should be kept down over both A and E strings.

b) As both the *Deil* and *Speed the Plough* require skill in rapid string-crossings, practise the following, keeping the bowing arm (fingers, wrist and forearm) flexible:

Ex. 5

Speed the Plough

Reel ♩ = 128

This tune, sometimes known as *The Naval Pillar*, was composed around 1800 by a John Morehead (or Muirhead). It could well have a connection with a religious festival in the north of England called "God speed the plough".

   a) The unison is again featured in this tune, but it is here preceded (as is most often the case) by an acciaccatura. This constitutes one of the most ubiquitous fingerprints in Scottish traditional music, and has not gone unnoticed by those wishing to parody the style.

   b) The up-bow conclusion to the 1st and 2nd measures of this reel not only prepares for the succeeding down-bow, but is a stylistic feature of this music.

Mr Alexander Laing's Hornpipe — Leuchold

Hornpipe Wm. Marshall

This hornpipe from Marshall's *Scottish Airs and Melodies* of 1822 illustrates a well-worn tradition of calling a tune after the dedicatee. Although this tune appears in Marshall's Collection in ¢ time, the more modern $\frac{2}{4}$ notation has been employed here, as it is felt to give a better idea of the pulse.

KEY:— E MAJOR

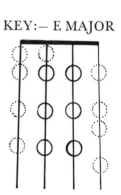

Charles Sutherland

Reel

Spiritedly

J. Murdoch Henderson

A prominent Fraserburgh violinist and disciple of J. Scott Skinner, Charles Sutherland was the proud possessor of a particularly fine Stradivarius violin — the "Goddard" Strad. This tune comes from Henderson's *Flowers of Scottish Melody*.

CHAPTER TWO

Jigs

❋

Merrily Danced the Quaker's Wife

Jig

Sprightly

(music notation for "Merrily Danced the Quaker's Wife")

This tune appeared in the Gows' *Complete Repository* (Part II, 1802).

The use of the straight slur (see *The White Cockade*) introduces the concept of articulating one note from another by a momentary stopping of the bow. The related principle of *broken-slurring* (imitating the effect of taking separate bows in the one bow-stroke) is important in jig-playing. The notation is a slur and a dash under the detached note.

Ex. 6

My Wife's a Wanton Wee Thing

Jig

This first appeared c1751 in James Oswald's *Caledonian Pocket Companion* (Book 6) and was used by Burns for the song, *My Wife's a Winsome Wee Thing*. Although Burns was attracted to "the light horse gallop of the air", he cites it as typical of many Scottish tunes in its peculiar rhythms which present the poet with "almost insuperable difficulties". This set is taken from Book II of Mackenzie's *Dance Music of Scotland* (1845).

The Stool of Repentance

Jig

The "stool of repentance" could well have been the fate of a "wanton wife" for, in the days when Presbyterianism was at its height, the "kirk session" punished adultery by having the wrongdoer sit for a number of Sundays in front of the assembled congregation. Repentance however is not an emotion which springs to mind when listening to this swaggering, confident tune. This set is taken from Davie's *Caledonian Repository* (Book I, 1829).

A form of ornamentation known as the *upper mordent* features in bars 3, 4, 8 and 16. This consists of the principal note, the note above and the principal note — the first two notes are played before the beat with the accent falling on the final note.

Ex. 7

written   played

Dunkeld House

Jig

Lively

This comes from Niel Gow's *First Collection of Strathspey Reels* (1784). The beautiful Perthshire village of Dunkeld lies no more than a stone's throw from Inver, birthplace of the great Niel Gow. Gow lies at rest in the churchyard of Little Dunkeld.

Se' n' Riogh a' tha aguin is fear linn.
(Wha'll be King but Charley)

Jig

Moderately

This is taken from Simon Fraser's great *Knockie* collection of *Airs and Melodies peculiar to the Highlands of Scotland and the Isles* (1816). The editor comments, "This is a melody common to Ireland, as well as to the Highlands of Scotland (having been known in this country since the 1745 as one of the incentives of rebellion) — but the melody is simple and beautiful, assimilating itself very much to the stile [*sic.*] of either".

KEY:— C MAJOR

In modern Gaelic this would be *'Se 'n Rìgh a th' againn fhearr linn* meaning "It is the king we have that we prefer".

a) As the ear would quickly tire of the exclusive broken-slurred approach to ⁶⁄₈ rhythms — the *bowed-out* method is also included here.

b) A form of ornamentation known as the *slide* features in bars 4 and 12. This is a group of notes played before the beat in ascending diatonic order to the principal note which retains the accent.

Ex. 8

written   played

44

Comma leam fein a Ministair
(What care I for the Minister)

Jig

Moderately

This "slip-jig" (as such a tune in $\frac{9}{8}$ time is called) is also taken from the "Knockie" collection. Turning again to Fraser's appendix we read, "The highlanders, it would seem, were as much inclined as others to resist the authority assumed by the clergy . . . . and they felt particularly sore upon this point if the clergyman was a worthless person himself".

The modern Gaelic orthography for this title would be *Coma leam fhéin am Ministear*.

CHAPTER THREE

The Slow Air, Song Air and Pastoral

Pentland Hills

This set is taken from Davie's *Caledonian Repository* (Book I, 2nd Series, 1850) and is therein attributed to James Oswald (c1710 - 1769). Oswald deserves a special mention in this collection as the author of the *Caledonian Pocket Companion*. Published between the years 1740 and 1769, this ran to twelve volumes, containing 500 tunes, of which about 40 were of his own composition. Oswald, who hailed from Dunfermline, lived variously in Edinburgh and (from 1741) in London, making his name as a dancing master, singer, composer and publisher.

a) The dotted quaver followed by the semiquaver () is one of the most characteristic rhythmic units in Scottish traditional music. Slurring is the simplest way of bowing this rhythm.

(i) Do not let the uneven rhythm upset the smoothness of the bowing.

(ii) Avoid the tendency for ♪♫ to become ♩₃♪. Stress the length of the dotted quaver and the brevity of the semiquaver.

b) Eighteenth century editions of this tune employ a form of ornamentation known as the *appoggiatura* (leaning note). The *appoggiatura* takes half the time value of the principal note.

Ex. 9
bar 16

18th cent. notation   played

A knowledge of the *appoggiatura* is invaluable to the study of the great 18th - early 19th century fiddle-collections such as those of the Gows and Marshall.

Mrs Janet B. Hardie

Alastair J. Hardie

Pastoral
Slow and dignified

47

a) Applying the principle and notation of broken-slurred bowing (see the section on Jigs) to the dotted quaver and semiquaver () produces what J. Murdoch Henderson in the *Flowers of Scottish Melody* refers to as "cross-cut sawing". It will help to think of the semiquaver not as an appendage to the **preceding** dotted quaver but as an anticipation of the **following** dotted quaver ( ). Practise the following, starting (i) with a down-bow; (ii) with an up-bow.

Ex. 10

b) *Cross-cut sawing* should not be seen as an end in itself, but as a step towards the mastery of *snap-bowing*. This relies for its effect on the written semiquaver being performed as a demisemiquaver, preceded by a demisemiquaver rest. This very short detached note is then said to be *kicked*. (The straight slur is again employed to denote the use of this stroke):—

Ex. 11

written   played

The ability to master *snap-bowing* cannot be too highly stressed, for, without it, an authentic rendition of the slow strathspey, dance-strathspey and Schottische is impossible.

c) A form of ornamentation known as the *turn* features in bar 2. In this case it consists of the note above, the principal note and the note below and, as can be seen from the placing of the sign (∞), is played **between** the third and fourth beats.

Ex. 12

written   played

48

Lady Jane Taylor's Strathspey — of Rothiemay

Pastoral
With dignity

Wm. Marshall
As played by A.J.H.

This pastoral comes from Marshall's 1822 Collection. Rothiemay, not far from the town of Huntly, is situated in the Strathbogie district of Aberdeenshire.

The syncopated rhythm ♪♪♪♫ (as in bar 2) is of considerable importance here. It may help to think of it as ♪♪ ♫ .

The Music o' Spey

Song Air

Sustained ♩ = 58-63

J. Scott Skinner

This song air first appeared in Skinner's *Miller o' Hirn Collection* (1881) in the key of **C** major. An editorial footnote, "when sung transpose it into A major" anticipates the set quoted above which comes from Skinner's *The Scottish Violinist* (1900).

a) The semiquaver followed by the dotted quaver () is an important feature of the above tune. An accent on the semiquaver  is essential to the idiomatic rendition of this rhythm.

b) The embellishment in bar 12 should be performed as follows:—

Gin ye kiss my Wife, I'll tell the Minister

From the *Harp and Claymore Collection* this "antiquarian melody" was communicated to Skinner by a Mr. John Stuart of Keith in Banffshire. Written here as a pastoral, this was originally a tune for the *Sean Triubhas*, an ancient highland dance where the sporran and kilt are replaced by tartan trews.

Taking a down-bow on the semiquaver and an up-bow on the dotted quaver, although technically more difficult than slurring, undoubtedly brings out the full character of this strong rhythm. This stroke, the *Scottish snap*, is best executed in the upper half of the bow with an accent on the semiquaver.

Lift the bow off the string after the dotted quaver of the *Scottish snap*. This will allow the open A-string to reverberate and simultaneously capture the correct phrasing.

Sword Dance

Strathspey tempo
Spiritedly

As played by J. Scott Skinner

This appears in Niel Gow's *First Collection of Strathspey Reels* under the title *Tail Toddle*, but is better known elsewhere as *Ghillie Callum*. The above set is from *The Scottish Violinist*.

One of the characteristics of the Scottish bagpipe is that it cannot play the note G♯. This tune is cast in the "pipe-mode", i.e., it employs the tonality of A, but with a flattened leading note (G♮). In violin terms therefore the fingerings are those for the key of D major.

a) When the *Scottish snap* is played in dance tempo as here, lift the bow smartly off the string on the second note. ♪♫. is therefore performed as: ♫↑

Ex. 14

b) *Hack-bowing*. The performance of the dotted quaver-semiquaver rhythm on separate down - up strokes ⊓∨ is employed in bars 4, 12 and 16.

Da Sixereen

Slow Reel or Hornpipe ♩ = 84

Tom Anderson

Tom Anderson (1910 - 1991) was born in Eshaness on the north-western mainland of Shetland. Widely known as a player, composer, teacher and authority on the music of his native Shetland, Tom was a tireless worker in the cause of traditional music.

The Sixereen is the Shetland six-oared open boat shaped like a Norse galley. Tom composed this tune in 1947, while watching this vessel crossing the bay.

In contrast to the previous tune the *Scottish snaps* are here played in a much more legato, on-the-string style.

CHAPTER FOUR

The Strathspey (Pt. I)

Whistle o'er the Lave o't

Slowish Strathspey ♩ = 116

Attr. to John Bruce

John Bruce (c1720 - 1785) has also been credited with the air *O Whistle and I'll come to you my Lad*. Burns, who referred to the Dumfries fiddler as "an honest man, though a red wud Highlander", produced a humorous setting of this tune for Johnson's *Musical Museum* (1787). In common with *Gin ye kiss my Wife*, the tune was used for the *Sean Triubhas*. This set is taken from Henderson's *Flowers of Scottish Melody*.

a) *Swinging-bow* is a feature of bars 5 and 9. This unites the slur and the snap-bow and can give a breadth to the phrasing, camouflaging the incessant four in a bar. This stroke demands whole-bows culminating in a *kicked* semiquaver.

Ex. 15

b) In bars 1 and 3 the slurred rhythm ♪♩. occurs on the **weaker** beats (2 and 4). The dance band practice of slurring this rhythm on the **strong** beats (1 and 3) is to be avoided.

The Miller o' Dervil

This tune is also known variously as *Benholm Castle*, *Bob Steele*, *Johnnie Steele*, *The Auld Brig o'Ayr* and *The New Brig o'Dee*. Although many people have had a hand in shaping it, the name principally associated with it is that of James Barnett of Kirkwall (1847 - 1898), whose *Johnnie Steele* was published in Book II of **Köhlers'** *Violin Repository*.

Bars 2 and 8 feature the use of *hack-bowing* (see *Sword Dance*). Although "hacking" ought to be avoided as a basic principle of strathspey-bowing, it can be effective when used sparingly.

Sir Harry's Welcome Home

Peter Hardie of Dunkeld in Perthshire (c 1775 - 1863) (see illustration on page 15) is principally remembered as a violin-maker, but this fine strathspey shows him to have been no mean composer.

This tune celebrates the homecoming of Sir Harry Niven-Lumsden, Bart., of Auchindoir, Perthshire.

a) The *syncopated triplet* ♪♫♪ features in bars 4, 8 and 16. Use a tiny bit of bow for the final (D) semiquaver.

b) Bars 4, 8 and 16 employ a form of notation known as the *Loop* (⌣). In the *Miller o' Hirn Collection* Skinner writes, "the loop is used only at the termination of a strain, the bow being dragged along, generally in a down bow".

Some commentators have argued that the loop "simply equals the tie" — but, if that is the case, why bother to devise a new form of notation in the first place?

The tie is altogether too suave and civilised for the irresistible rhythmic impetus of the strathspey and slow strathspey. The loop is therefore used (on the down- and up-strokes) and denotes that the *tied* note be given a certain degree of re-emphasis.

There is surely a link between the loop notation and the tendency of many traditional players who, instead of "phrasing-off", end a tune with an accented flourish.

Forbes Morrison

Forbes Morrison (1833 - 1906) of Tarves in Aberdeenshire was particularly noted for his expertise in performing the syncopated triplet. Like Skinner himself, he combined the professions of fiddler and dancing master. The written-out reprise of the first measure (or section) conforms to Skinner's interpretation on disc and is not a feature of the original version in the *Logie Collection*. Although not indicated as such, the alternative ending to the tune could be regarded as a second-time bar when the tune is repeated. (The upper notes would constitute the first-time bar, the lower notes the second.*)

Dotted-rhythm back-bowing is a feature of bars 1, 3, 5 and 7. This stroke, known to the classical violinist as the *polonaise-hook*, is executed in the upper third of the bow. Reverse the pattern used for hack-bowing, *i.e.,* take the dotted quaver on an up-bow (⌐). Its effectiveness is in direct proportion to the infrequency of its use.

Tulchan Lodge

J. Scott Skinner

Tulchan Lodge, near Advie in Speyside, was the Scottish home of a certain Lady Chetwode, and it was here that she and her family had dancing lessons from the youthful J. Scott Skinner. This tune first appeared in the *Logie Collection*.
  a) Point the subtle difference between the ♫♩ and ♩♫♩ rhythms in bar 12.
  b) The grace notes in bar 14 are simply a different way of notating the mordent (see *The Stool of Repentance*).

CHAPTER FIVE

The Flat Keys

The Marquis o' Huntly's Snuff Mull

KEY:— F MAJOR

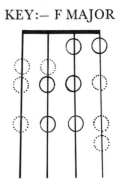

This is a celebrated example of the Gows' habit of stealing other people's tunes. It appeared in Niel Gow's *Fourth Collection of Strathspey Reels* (1800) but was based on the air *Miss Dallas* from William Marshall's 1781 collection.

The sign ⌒ (penultimate bar) indicates a pause *i.e.*, the sound is prolonged to a length left to the discretion of the player.

John Roy Stewart

Strathspey

Alex McGlashan

From his rather extravagant style of dress, Alexander McGlashan (1740 - 1797) acquired the name "King" McGlashan. He has the two-fold distinction of having taught Nathaniel Gow the violin and of having employed him as a 'cellist in his band.

This tune comes from *A Collection of Strathspey Reels* (1780). McGlashan published two other collections in 1781 and 1786.

John Roy Stewart, a descendant of "The Wolf of Badenoch", was a Jacobite agent and had the distinction of being the last person to be knighted by the Old Pretender.

The New Brig o' Methlick

Reel

William Hardie

The Aberdeenshire village of Methlick is situated on the river Ythan. As the bridge in question was completed in 1844, the composition of this reel and its companion strathspey (see Chap. 6) can be dated around the middle of the 19th century.

This set is based on the version published in Henderson's *Flowers of Scottish Melody*.

The above three F-major tunes constitute a *Group*, *i.e.*, a suite or set of tunes which combine to form a satisfying whole. *Groups* can comprise two, three or more tunes and are related by constraints of key, style and tempo. Possible combinations include slow air, strathspey and reel; march, strathspey and reel; slow strathspey and reel; hornpipes and reels, *etc.*

All the tunes in the sections on The Minor Mode (Parts I and II) are set out in *groups* (one *group* per key).

The Shakins o' the Pocky

Solo Strathspey
Boldly accented

P. Milne & J. Scott Skinner
As played by Aly Bain

Peter Milne (1824 - 1908), the "Tarland Minstrel", was, according to his illustrious pupil J. Scott Skinner, "one of the finest native musicians that Scotland ever produced". He earned his livelihood as a theatre-violinist and, before the building of the road bridge, by entertaining the passengers on the ferry boats plying across the River Forth.

Although much of the material in this collection has been refined by different hands down the years, it is unusual to find a tune such as the above composed as a result of a direct collaboration. From the *Miller o' Hirn Collection*, this tune takes its title from the fact that, at one stage, the two friends were so impoverished that they had to club their meagre resources together just to afford the price of one dram.

KEY:— Bb MAJOR

The turn at the beginning of this tune is played before the beat:

written   played

Aly Bain was born in Lerwick, Shetland, and from the age of 14 came under the influence of fellow Shetlander Tom Anderson. The recordings of Bill Hardie, Hector MacAndrew and J. Scott Skinner have also helped to mould his style. From 1972 Aly has been the fiddler with the renowned traditional folk band "The Boys of the Lough" and in this capacity has toured throughout Britain, Europe and the United States.

Mrs Forbes Leith

Reel

First appearing in Skinner's *Thirty New Strathspeys and Reels* of 1868 and subsequently in the *Miller o'Hirn Collection*, this makes an excellent reel to follow either *The Shakins o'the Pocky* or *The Firth House*. This set is taken from Henderson's *Flowers of Scottish Melody*.

The Firth House

Hornpipe

This is taken, as are the two following tunes, from that great source of fine hornpipes, Köhlers' *Violin Repository* (1881 - 1885).

a) This tune demonstrates how the techniques of the strathspey (*back-bowing*, *snap-bowing* and *swinging-bow*) can be applied to the hornpipe.

b) **D.C.** (*Da Capo*) **al fine** means "go back to the beginning and play until '*Fine*' " (the end).

The Newcastle Hornpipe

Hornpipe

J. Hill

Although a native of Dundee, James Hill spent most of his life at Gateshead in the north-east of England. Apart from his many fine hornpipes, of which the *High Level* is probably the most famous, Hill is remembered as the composer of the strathspey *Earl Grey*.

Cross-bowing is featured here (as in bars 4 - 5). Bowing usually reinforces the normal rhythmic stresses in a bar (Ex 17a); cross-bowing subtly heightens these by a form of syncopation (Ex 17b).

The *legato* quality of cross-bowing is an important element in the hornpipe, contrasting as it does with the snap- and back-bowing.

Princess Beatrice

W. B. Laybourn

As played by Aly Bain

Hornpipe

W.B. Laybourn (1835 - 1886) was born in London, but spent thirteen years in North Shields (significantly, considering the hornpipe's Newcastle connection) before settling in Edinburgh. He edited Köhlers' *Violin Repository* (this tune comes from Book III), contributing sixteen hornpipes of his own composition. This set comes from Henderson's *Flowers of Scottish Melody*.

The double-stopping provided by the bracketed note is played only at the conclusion of the piece; see also the opening piece of Chapter eight, page 78.

The Methlick Style

As played by A.J.H.

KEY:— E♭ MAJOR

This air was communicated to Bill Hardie by his grandfather, William Hardie Jnr., of Methlick (c 1856 - 1944 — see photograph on page 16). A form of ornamentation known as the *arpeggio* features in bars 9, 13 and 17. This consists of the notes of a chord usually sounded in ascending order and played before the beat:—

Ex. 18

written   played

64

The Glories of 'The Star'

Solo Strathspey
Pointedly

J. Scott Skinner

Taken from the *Elgin Collection of Scotch Music* (1884), this tune is dedicated to a Mrs. Fraser, the proprietrix of The Star public house in Nairn.

The arpeggios in bars 7 and 9 and the slide in bar 11 are all played before the beat.

The Trumpet

Hornpipe

As played by Bill Hardie

The broken-chord writing and the quasi-triple tongued triplets suggest that this fine hornpipe was inspired by the trumpet fanfare. It appears in Book I of Köhlers' *Violin Repository*.

Play the triplet semiquavers with the minimum amount of bow (upper third of the stick), accenting the first note of each group.

CHAPTER SIX

The Strathspey (Pt. II)

The Dean Brig o' Edinburgh

Slow Strathspey
Distinctly accented

Archie Allan
Var. by J. F. Dickie

VAR.

The original title of this tune was *Miss Gray of Carse*. Claimed as the work of the Rev. Mr. Tough of Kinnoul, it appeared under its present title in Davie's *Caledonian Repository*. Peter Milne made a speciality of this tune (Middleton's *Selection of Strathspeys*, c1885, actually makes the mistake of attributing it to him). The credit for composing this classic slow strathspey however goes to Archie Allan of Forfar (1794 - 1831).

The stylish variations to this air and to *Master Francis Sitwell* are the work of "the shy genius of the strathspey", James F. Dickie (1886 - 1982). Born in Aberdeenshire in the village of Old Deer, Dickie was described by J. Murdoch Henderson as "a player of great taste and polish, his rendering of E♭ airs and slow strathspeys being inimitable".

The *up-driven bow* (♫.♩.♪) is a prominent feature of this tune (as in bar 1). It gets its name from the fact that the second note of the up-bow is accented by means of increased bow-travel and pressure. Take the initial semiquaver near the point of the bow, leaving a whole bow for the following three notes. *Kick* the final semiquaver.

According to contemporary reports this was the stroke which gave such breadth to Niel Gow's playing. Skinner alludes to this in his *Miller o' Hirn Collection*, "The accented up-bow, so powerful in the hand of the famous Niel Gow . . . has been carefully considered and the arrow has been introduced in explanation of that difficult peculiarity of strathspey playing".

This "arrow" notation ♫.♩.♪ , employed throughout the *Miller o' Hirn Collection*, is normally now abbreviated to a straight line joining the final three notes, a practice adopted throughout the present book.

A form of the up-driven bow is often used in association with the turn (as in bars 2 and 4). The inclusion of the natural ♮ means that the lower note is raised by a semitone from A♭ to A♮ (E♭ to E♮ in the case of bars 4 and 12).

Ex. 19

written   played

Master Francis Sitwell

Slow Strathspey
Elegantly

Nath. Gow
Variations by J. F. Dickie

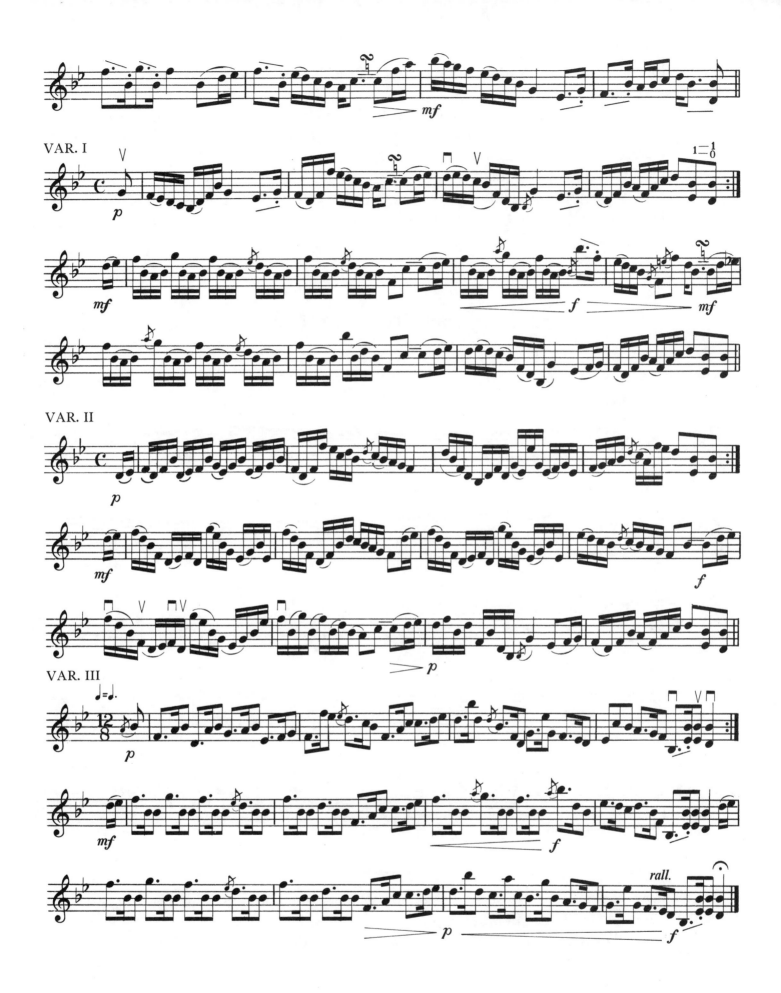

VAR. I

VAR. II

VAR. III

69

This slow strathspey by Nathaniel Gow comes from Niel Gow's *Fourth Collection of Strathspey Reels* (1800).

a) In order to prevent running out of bow, the initial semiquaver of the figuration (2nd measure of Var. I) should be given as much bow as the following three slurred notes. The resultant accent on the down bow is stylistic and quite in keeping with the character of the music.

b) The lilt in Var. III will be conveyed by stroking the dotted quavers and using very short bows on the following semiquavers.

The New Brig o' Methlick

Taken from Henderson's *Flowers of Scottish Melody*, this is the matching strathspey to the same composer's *New Brig o' Methlick* reel.

The letters DS (Dal Segno) at the end of the first time bar indicate that the repeat is to take place from the sign 𝄋.

The Marquis of Huntly's Farewell

Wm. Marshall
As played by J. Scott Skinner

Skinner's performance of this gained him first place at a competition held in Inverness in September 1863. This set is based on the version from the *Harp and Claymore Collection*.

a) This tune features *down-driven bow* ( ) (as in bar 2). Stop the bow between the crotchet and the semiquaver and perform the semiquaver (firmly accented) and dotted quaver in the normal *Scottish-snap* style.

    As with the up-driven bow, this stroke is frequently used in association with the turn (bars 1, 3 and 5). Here the dotted quaver is accented by means of increased bow-travel and pressure, the final semiquaver being *kicked*.

b) The notation adopted here for the turn is that employed by Skinner in the *Harp and Claymore*.

Ex. 20

written   played

c) The use of *half-position* will accommodate the G♯ in this passage. Move the hand back to the nut and play the G♯ with a 1st finger, the A with a 2nd and the B with a 3rd. Resume 1st position on the semiquaver D.

Mr A. G. Wilken's Favourite

Solo Strathspey
With expression

J. Scott Skinner
As played by Bill Hardie

This "solo strathspey" and the following two dance strathspeys are taken from the *Miller o' Hirn Collection*. The Mr. Wilken in question was an amateur violinist from the Aberdeenshire village of Ellon.

Mrs Chree

Highland Schottische or Strathspey

J. Scott Skinner

As Mrs. Chree resided at the Schoolhouse, Keig in Aberdeenshire, she was, presumably, a schoolmaster's wife.

The Miller o' Hirn

Schottische or Strathspey ♩ = 140

J. Scott Skinner

The "Strathspey King" was confident enough to believe that this, the opening tune from the collection of the same name, would outshine the celebrated *Miller o' Drone* strathspey:

> We'll 'Drone' nae mair, sin' we ha'e got
> The 'Miller o' the Hirn', O.

The Laird o' Drumblair

Strathspey or Schottische ♩ = 148

J. Scott Skinner
As played by Bill Hardie

William F. McHardy, the Laird of Drumblair, was a friend and benefactor of Skinner's. Characteristically the composer requests that this tune, one of the most celebrated of all dance strathspeys, be played "with fire and force". It was published in the *Harp and Claymore Collection*.

a) Bars 2 and 6 show the application of cross-bowing techniques to the strathspey (see *The Newcastle Hornpipe*).

b) The open A-string, sounding throughout these two bars, is an easy and effective form of chord-playing.

Glenlivet

J. Scott Skinner
As played by Bill Hardie

Strathspey or Highland Schottische

Scott Skinner's made anither tune
The very dirl o't reached the moon
Till ilka lassie an' her loon
Commenced to dance fu' frisky O.

These lines preface the appearance of this spirited strathspey from the *Elgin Collection* which toasts one of the more famous brands of Scottish proprietary malt whisky. The tune is alternatively known as the *Minmore Schottische*.

Bar 5 demonstrates a more expansive treatment of strathspey cross-bowing.

CHAPTER SEVEN

Birlin' Reels

James Hardie

Reel

J. Scott Skinner

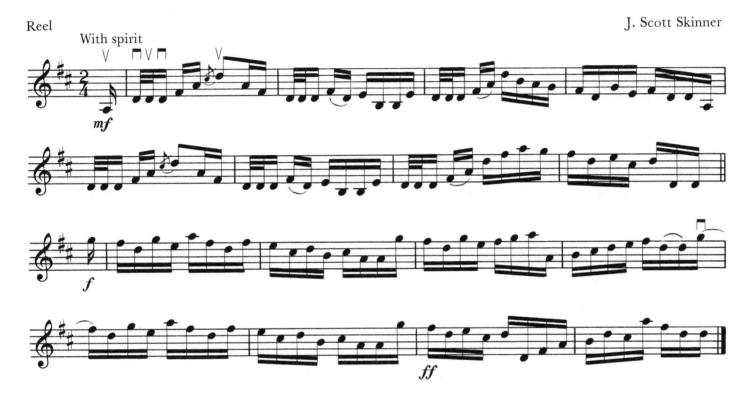

J. Scott Skinner, the greatest fiddler/composer of his generation, here pays tribute to one of the most distinguished contemporary violin makers. Indeed, Scottish traditional fiddle-players and fiddle-makers have long had a close, mutually supportive relationship.

From the *Harp and Claymore Collection*, this reel was written specifically to follow the strathspey *The Miller o'Dervil*.

Birlin'-notes are a feature of this reel (bars 1 - 3 and 5 - 7). This rhythmic embellishment consists of three notes of the same pitch (or   ). Executed at the point of the bow with a quivering movement of the hand, the stroke could be likened to an abbreviated form of the tremolando (the rapid reiteration of a note particularly associated with orchestral string writing).

Practise the following a) slowly (♩ = 80), b) at a quick tempo (♩ = 126) with a slight stiffening of the right fore-arm for the *birlin'-notes*.

Ex. 21

Da Grocer

Reel ♩ = 106

Tom Anderson

Composed in June, 1952, this good-going Shetland reel is dedicated to Mr. Willie Birnie, an excellent piper and traditional music enthusiast.

The Burn o' Forgue

Reel

With enthusiasm

J. Scott Skinner

The parish of Forgue is situated in Aberdeenshire between the towns of Huntly and Turriff. Published in J. Scott Skinner's *Logie Collection*, this makes an ideal reel to follow the strathspey *Tulchan Lodge*.

Jenny Hardie's Reel

Reel

Neatly and with Spirit

Bill Hardie

Bill Hardie dedicated this spirited reel to his late wife, Mrs. Janet B. Hardie (neé Kennedy, 1912-78), who was a native of the village of Auckengill, near Wick in Caithness.

CHAPTER EIGHT

Third Position and Position-changing

Robert Innes of Stirling University

Stirling University has for many years been the venue for an annual Scots Fiddle Summer School. This pioneer venture was jointly established in 1978 by the late Robert Innes, the University's then Director of Continuing Education and Shetland fiddler Tom Anderson. The teaching staff has included such distinguished players as Aly Bain, Angus Grant, Bill Hardie and Jack Stuart.

This tune is playable, throughout, in *third position*. Play Ex. 22 in 1st position:—

Move the hand up the neck of the violin until the 1st finger sounds the note G. Check the intonation by playing this note together with the open G string.

In the tune and Ex. 23, 3rd and 4th fingers are close together.

Ex. 23

Remember that the higher the notes are pitched, the closer they lie to one another on the fingerboard. Make an allowance for this by placing the fingers a little more closely together.

The Duchess Tree

Song Air

Slow and sustained ♩ = 63-66

J. Scott Skinner

This first appeared in the *Logie Collection* as a song to words by William Martin, composer of the following strathspey. When it subsequently appeared in *The Scottish Violinist*, Skinner transposed it from A flat to A major.

Natural harmonics are a feature of this tune (bars 3, 7, 11 and 15.). They are indicated by a circle placed above the note. If, instead of depressing the string on to the fingerboard, the finger rests lightly at various key-points along its length, flute-like notes (harmonics) will result.

Octave-harmonics are the most common and are produced in 3rd position with an upward extension of the 4th finger, the pad lightly touching the string.

Remember that only the finger executing the harmonic may touch the string.

Ex. 24

William Duguid — Fyvie

William Martin (1836 - 1908) was a man of many parts: a teacher by profession but also an able fiddler, composer and poet. His gifts in the latter respect found expression in lyrics to many of Skinner's melodies, of which the most notable were those to *The Bonnie Lass o' Bon-Accord*.

William Duguid (1866 - 1905) was reputedly "one of J. Scott Skinner's ablest disciples". His influence extends down to the present day through the recordings of his most distinguished pupil, James F. Dickie (see appendix discography). This set comes from Henderson's *Flowers of Scottish Melody*.

a) 1st and 3rd positions are required here. *Position-changing* (Method I) is facilitated by means of open-strings. The principle is best illustrated by the arpeggio of A major.

Ex. 25

Ascending—   While playing the open E the hand/arm moves from 1st to 3rd positions in readiness for the 1st finger A.

Descending—   While playing the open E the hand/arm moves from 3rd to 1st position in readiness for the 2nd finger C♯.

Two golden rules for position changing are i) avoid gripping with the thumb; ii) hold the violin securely between shoulder and jaw.

b) **The G♯s in bars 7 and 11 are played in 3rd position with a 1st finger backward extension. The crotchet-E at the end of bar 9 is treated as a harmonic.**

Pittengardener's Rant

J. Scott Skinner

On the manuscript of this particular tune (the facsimile is reproduced on page 21) Skinner writes "these rants require physical force — plenty of go".

Pittengardener, described by the composer as "one of the most successful 'Men o'the Mearns', reamin' fu' o' music", was one of the best pupils of William Skinner, the violinist's father. This tune was published in the *Harp and Claymore Collection*.

Position-changing (Method II). In the ascending scale-passage (2nd time bar) the change from 1st to 3rd position is effected by the 1st finger executing a slide or *glissando*.

The speed at which this manoeuvre is executed will render the *glissando* and *guide note* (♪) inaudible.

Charlie Hardie

Reel

J. Scott Skinner

This reel from the *Miller o' Hirn Collection* provides further evidence of the regard which J. Scott Skinner had for the musical abilities of the Hardie family. Apart from his admiration for Charles Hardie's violinistic skills, Skinner was in the habit of submitting to him his compositions for advice and criticism prior to publication.

The Bonnie Lass o' Bon-Accord

Violin Solo

Moderato ♩ = 84

J. Scott Skinner

VAR. I

VAR. II

Sadly

Apart from being composed in Aberdeen (December, 1884) this celebrated "solo, song, or marching air" has many other connections with that city. Skinner met the bonnie lass in question, a certain Wilhelmina Bell, at a party in Aberdeen. "Bon-Accord" is the motto of the city and the opening bars of the tune even appear on Skinner's gravestone in the city's Allenvale cemetery.

Variation form is an important part of the fiddler/composer's craft. In a footnote to this tune from the *Logie Collection*, Skinner says:

> Nothing has such fascinating interest to an accomplished composer as writing variations. He is enabled to draw from the theme all possible conclusions and to evolve various beauties from the sometimes meagre and insignificant looking theme.

a) *Position-changing* (Method III). Here the change from 1st to 3rd is facilitated with the same finger: 1 — 1 in bars 4, 8, 11, 12, 16 and 20; 2 — 2 in bars 24 and 36; 4 — 4 (harmonic) in bars 23 and 35.

   The glissando-effect observed previously will be more pronounced in this type of position-change. Take the type and period of the tune into account when using the glissando. The slow strathspeys and pastorals of Skinner, for example, lend themselves to a more pronounced use of this device than those of the Gows, Fraser and Marshall.

b) With the exception of the F♯s and G♯s, the fingering in Var. II (up to the C♯ quaver in the 3rd from last bar) will be that for the key of C major.

CHAPTER NINE

The Minor Mode (Pt. I)

The Braes o' Bushbie

A favourite of Niel Gow's, this slow march was published in Vol I of J. McFadyen's *Repository of Scots and Irish Airs* (c1795). This set is taken from Henderson's *Flowers of Scottish Melody*.

This and the following strathspey and reel are in the key of G-minor. (B♭ is the relative-major.) The finger patterns for minor keys are those for their relative majors with the exception of some accidentals inherent in the concept of the minor scale.

KEY:– G MINOR

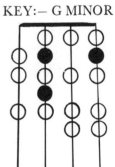

In the harmonic version of the minor scale the 7th degree is sharpened by a semitone and in the melodic version the 6th and 7th degrees are similarly sharpened (in ascending passages only). The fingering-charts for the minor keys will distinguish between the basic fingerings and those involving accidentals by having the latter shaded in except in the case of the E♮, A♮ and D♮ which fall on open strings.

The Marquis of Huntly's Strathspey

Wm. Marshall

Strathspey

This first appeared in Marshall's 1781 *Collection of Strathspey Reels* as the *Marquis of Huntly's Reel*, assuming its present title in the 1822 collection.

Bar 12 of the 1822 version of the tune demonstrates the use of the *doodle* (the grouping together of four notes of the same pitch):—

Ex. 28

This 18th century fingerprint has now fallen out of favour, modern players tending to substitute a simpler alternative such as that demonstrated in the above set. It should be noted here that the sharpened F immediately preceding the ornament also provides for an F♯ inflection in the turn.

The Strathbogie Toast

Reel

Wm. Marshall

Huntly is the principal town of the Aberdeenshire district of Strathbogie. This reel, also taken from the 1822 Collection, makes a spirited conclusion to the preceding slow march and strathspey.

Nathaniel Gow's Lament for the Death of his Brother

Lament

Nath. Gow

Slow and with pathos ♩· = 40

87

A player of "bold and spirited style", William Gow, eldest son of the famous Niel, died in 1791 at the age of forty. Taken from the *Third Collection of Strathspey Reels* (1792), Nathaniel's tribute to his brother is written in a similar vein to the celebrated *Niel Gow's Lament for the Death of his Second Wife.*

KEY:– A MINOR
RELATIVE MAJOR:– C

The Banks of Spey

Strathspey

Wm. Marshall

This Marshall composition reminds us that the strathspey is traditionally believed to have originated in the Spey valley of north-eastern Scotland. Angus Cumming, last in the line of a celebrated family of 18th century fiddlers from Strathspey, was perhaps nearer the mark when he said that the Spey valley was the area where the strathspey had been "preserved in the greatest purity".

a) *Triple-stopping*, a term describing chords composed of 3 notes, is a feature of bars 1 and 3 (Ex. 29 (i)); further possible triple-stopped chords, in C, G, D and A are also shown (Ex. 29 (ii)), the minor inflections being given in brackets.

Ex. 29 i)   ii)

written   played

b) It is often appropriate to conclude a group with a chord. As Skinner says in the *Miller o' Hirn Collection*: "When closing a tune, the chord of the key should be given, as many strathspeys and reels do not end on the key but frequently on the fifth".

88

The turn in bars 4 and 12 is performed as follows:

Ex. 30

Mr Edward Wagstaff's Fancy

Reel

Wm. Marshall

Like *The Banks of Spey*, this C major reel comes from Marshall's 1822 collection. The move from minor to relative major gives good tonal contrast and a bright conclusion to the group.

The second measure of this tune employs *back-bowing* (see *The East Neuk o' Fife*). The figuration in bars 10 and 14, crossing from a higher to a lower string, often lies easier when bowed in this manner.

Gu mo maidh a thig an crun dhuit a Thearluich oig
(Well may Charley wear the Crown)

Slow Air

Slowly and solemnly

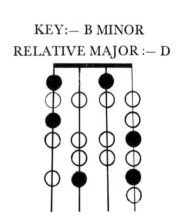

KEY:— B MINOR

RELATIVE MAJOR :— D

This air and the following strathspey come from Simon Fraser's *Knockie* Collection. The editor ironically comments:

> But so beautiful an air belonging to that period (the uprising of 1745) may now take the name of Charlotte in place of Charles and be associated with our sentiments of attachment to the present Royal Family.

The modern form of the above Gaelic title would be *Guma mhath a thig an crùn dhuit, a Thearlaich òig*, meaning literally *Well may the crown suit you, young Charles*.

The rising sharpened fourth of the scale (E♯) is easily effected by sharpening the first finger by a semitone. This note is not characteristic of B minor tunes.

*Stoileadh Nial Gobha
(Niel Gow's Style)

Strathspey

Simon Fraser

(*The present-day Gaelic spelling would be "Staoileadh Néill Ghobha")

On this strathspey Fraser remarks:

> "This is merely Niel Gow's sprightly stile [sic] imitated by the editor, in which his friends are pleased to say he has made a happy effort".

Reel

The Heiress

This air was attributed to Simon Fraser in Joseph Lowe's Collection, Book 6 (1844 - 1845). J. Murdoch Henderson, from whose *Flowers of Scottish Melody* this set is taken, was of the opinion, "this air matches Fraser's 'Niel Gow's Style' 1816 Coll.".

The bracketed introductory F♯ is played only if the tune is repeated.

The Marchioness of Huntly's Favorite

Slow Air

Slowly and with pathos ♩ = 46-48

Wm. Marshall

Marshall here honours the dedicatee of his 1822 *Scottish Airs and Melodies*. The Marchioness, Elizabeth Brodie (1794 - 1864) also gave her name to another two tunes, apart from this pastoral and jig. If this slow air was indeed one of the lady's favourite tunes, we applaud her taste, for Marshall has here produced one of his most memorable compositions.

KEY:— C MINOR
RELATIVE MAJOR:— E♭

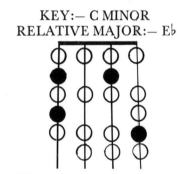

The Marchioness of Huntly's Favorite Jig

Jig

Lively

Wm. Marshall

92

CHAPTER TEN

The Higher Positions

Chapel Keithack

Wm. Marshall
As played by Hector MacAndrew

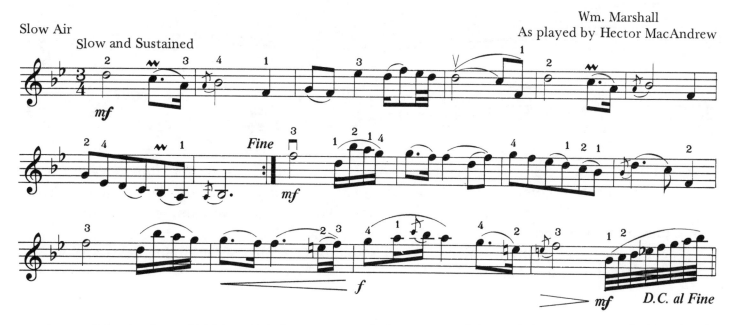

Hector MacAndrew (1903 - 1980) was one of the most celebrated interpreters of this classic Marshall slow air (1822 Collection). Born in the Aberdeenshire village of Fyvie, he inherited his talent from his father, a noted fiddler and piper, and his grandfather who was taught by a pupil of Niel Gow. As fiddler, composer and teacher, Hector held a position of pre-eminent respect and influence for over fifty years in the traditional music world.

With the exception of the concluding A — B♭, the first measure of this tune can be played (to good violinistic and musical effect) entirely in *second position*. Play Ex. 31 in 1st position.

Move the hand up the neck of the violin until the 1st finger sounds the note B♭. In Ex. 32, 3rd and 4th fingers are close together on the G and D strings, 2 and 3 on the A.

The House of Skene

Pastoral

With serenity ♩ = 46

James Davie

James Davie (1783 - 1857) of Aberdeen is chiefly remembered for his *Caledonian Repository*, a six-volume collection comprising 802 airs. This pastoral is taken from the final volume which was published in 1855. A music-seller by profession, Davie was also well-known in Aberdeen as a theatre-player and teacher.

Move into 2nd position on the second semiquaver of bar 8, resuming 1st position on the penultimate note of bar 9.

Harvey Mitchell

Pastoral

Alastair J. Hardie

Slowly and with dignity

Harvey Mitchell was Head of Cultural and International Services for Lothian Regional Council until the department was closed in 1981. He has been a generous friend to the cause of Scottish traditional fiddle music and his sympathetic attitude to the present book is gratefully acknowledged.

The upper register of the instrument is featured in the second measure of this tune, necessitating the use of *fourth position*. Play Ex. 33 in 1st position.

Move the hand up the neck of the fiddle until the 1st finger sounds the note E♭. In Ex. 34, 3rd and 4th fingers are close together.

Madge ("Farewell to Scotland")

Song Air

J. Scott Skinner

William Martin again wrote the words for this song from the *Logie Collection*. In this version from *The Scottish Violinist*, Skinner transposes the melody an octave higher.

Fifth position is used in bars 3, 8 to 9 and 14 to 16. In positions 1 to 4 the left hand/arm moves progressively up the neck of the violin with little change in the lateral position. From the 5th position upwards, however, the obstacle of the body of the instrument itself necessitates moving the arm considerably round to the right. The thumb is now more inclined to the horizontal with the ball in the niche where the neck joins the body. Play Ex. 35 in 3rd position.

95

Move the hand up the neck until the 1st finger sounds the note F♯. In Ex. 36, 2nd and 3rd fingers are close together on the A string, 1 and 2 on the E.

Ex. 36

Tarland Memories

Pastoral

Grandly ♩ = 60

Peter Milne

This, one of Peter Milne's last compositions, has the alternative title *George Rose Wood*. Wood was Skinner's chief concert agent from 1922 - 1925. This set is based on a version from Henderson's *Flowers of Scottish Melody*.

a) Bar 15 contains one note, the high G, which lies beyond the normal gamut of 5th position. This note can be produced by extending the 4th finger by a semitone. As the key is D major, 1st and 2nd fingers are now close together on the A and E strings:

Ex. 37

The Mathematician

Hornpipe

J. Scott Skinner

From the *Harp and Claymore Collection*, Skinner dedicated this tune to a Dr. Clark of Cairo.

The second measure of this hornpipe provides quite a challenge to left-hand technique. Apart from the use of positions 3 (bar 9), 4 (bars 10 - 11) and 5 (bars 12 - 13), *sixth position* is introduced at bars 14 - 15. Play Ex. 38 in 1st and then in 5th positions.

Keeping the thumb in the niche between the neck and body of the instrument, move the 1st finger up the fingerboard until the note G is produced. In Ex. 39, 3rd and 4th fingers are close together in second bar.

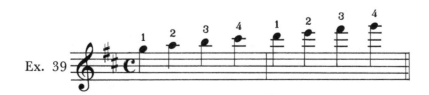

Haslam's Hornpipe

Hornpipe

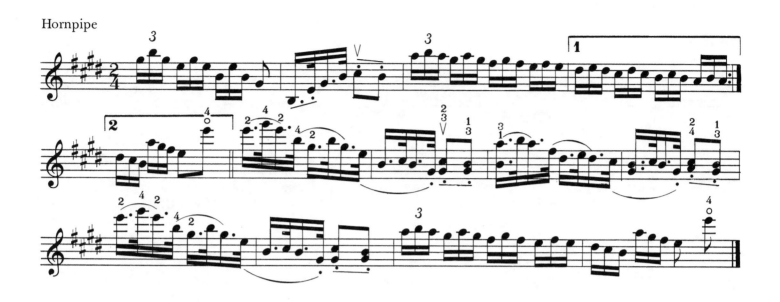

This is J. Murdoch Henderson's set from the *Flowers of Scottish Melody*, the tune originally coming from Köhlers' *Violin Repository*.

   a) Bars 6 and 10 again employ 6th position (2nd finger on E and 4th on G♯, see Ex. 40 i). Alternatively it is possible to play this passage in the 5th position, with the 3rd finger on the E and a 4th extension on the G♯ (Ex. 40ii).

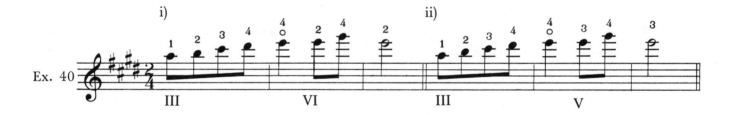

Ex. 40

   b) Bars 6 - 11 provide an example of the extended application of cross-bowing in the hornpipe.

Mar Castle

This pastoral comes from the *Harp and Claymore Collection*. Mar (of the title) is an ancient district of south west Aberdeenshire, subdivided into Braemar, Midmar and Cromar.

    a) *Seventh position* is featured here in the penultimate bar. Play Ex. 41 (i) in 5th position.

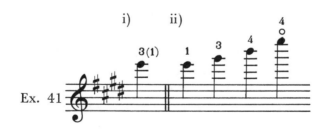

Keeping the thumb in the niche, move the 1st finger up until the note E is produced. In Ex. 41 (ii) the B is taken with a 4th finger extension and the top E is a harmonic, again taken with the 4th finger.

    b) The sequence of position-changing in the last 2 bars is indicated by Roman numerals.

CHAPTER ELEVEN

The Minor Mode (Pt. II)

Pennan Den

After spending his early years as a sailor and fisherman, James Watt (1832 - 1909) became a teacher in his native Pennan, a village a few miles along the coast from Fraserburgh. Although something of a violin-maker, his services were more in demand as a dance-fiddler. This tune, together with the following strathspey and reel, comes from the *Flowers of Scottish Melody* and was communicated to J. Murdoch Henderson by George Riddell.

The written-out turns (bars 2, 4, 10 and 12) are all played before the beat.

KEY:— D MINOR
RELATIVE MAJOR:— F

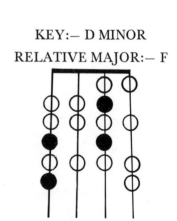

Gavin Greig

A Scottish Study

J. Murdoch Henderson

Gavin Greig (1856 - 1914), whom Henderson describes as "perhaps the most outstanding personality in Buchan in his day", was, like the composer, a schoolmaster. (Notice the prevalence of teaching as a profession amongst the Scottish fiddler-composer fraternity.)

Although Greig is best remembered as "one of the most successful and pertinacious researchers that have explored the realm of ballad literature" (he collected over 3000), he was also a poet, dramatist and musician. His abilities in this last capacity enabled him to act as a most efficient editor of Skinner's *Harp and Claymore Collection*.

George Riddell

Reel

J. Murdoch Henderson

George Riddell "a musician and composer of repute" belonged to Rosehearty, a fishing village just a few miles to the east of Pennan.

Roslin Castle

This is J. Murdoch Henderson's set from the *Flowers of Scottish Melody*. Although this appeared in the *Caledonian Pocket Companion* (Vol IV, 1752), it was not, as was long supposed, claimed by James Oswald. (Oswald usually affixed asterisks to his own compositions; there are none in this case.) The tune had already appeared in McGibbon's 2nd Collection of 1746 under the title *House of Glams*.

Roslin Castle stands on the north bank of the River Esk, a few miles south-west of Edinburgh.

KEY:— E MINOR
RELATIVE MAJOR:— G

Lady Cathrine Stewart's Strathspey

Strathspey

This comes from Niel Gow's *First Collection of Strathspey Reels*. The groups of 4 semiquavers in bars 6, 7, 10 and 12 appear in the original as ♪♩♩ — a further illustration of the *appoggiatura* and its interpretation.

As a thoiseach
(Keep it up)

Pipe Reel
Spiritedly

Commenting in his "Knockie" Collection on reels such as the above, Fraser states "ordinary performers on the violin are not ready to take them up, as they require a distinct bow to each note". This un-slurred *Detaché* style can be explained on the grounds of this being a "pipe reel".

Mrs Shearer of Buchromb

Pastoral

With pathos

Wm. Marshall

These two F-minor tunes come from the 1822 Collection. Buchromb is situated just north of Dufftown in Banffshire. One of the manifestations of Marshall's lively intellect lay in his readiness to experiment with the more difficult and remote major and minor keys.

KEY:— F MINOR
RELATIVE MAJOR:— A♭

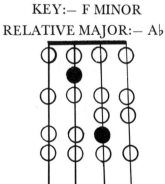

Hatton of Buchromb's Reel

Reel

Wm. Marshall

Considering the volatile nature of the fiddle-writing here, a north-east player might well describe this reel as "a double-breasted tune — going frae a' side o' the fiddle tae th'ither".

Ossian

There is a joy in grief — Ossian

Elegy

J. Scott Skinner

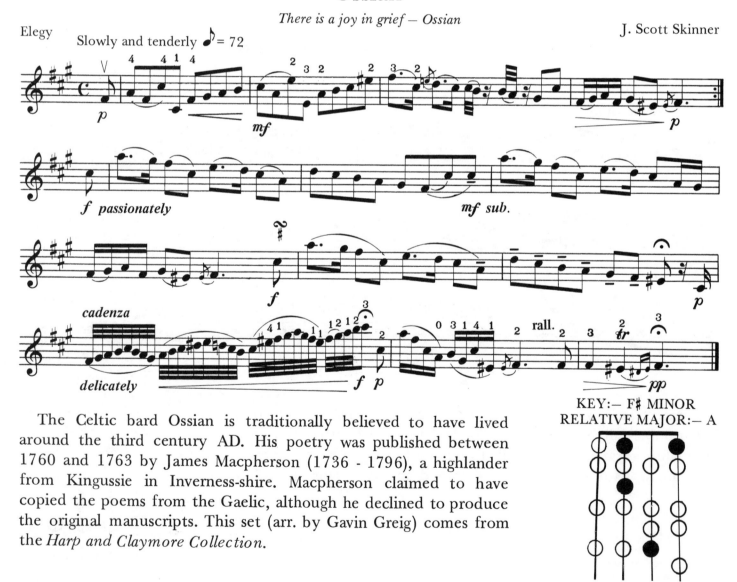

The Celtic bard Ossian is traditionally believed to have lived around the third century AD. His poetry was published between 1760 and 1763 by James Macpherson (1736 - 1796), a highlander from Kingussie in Inverness-shire. Macpherson claimed to have copied the poems from the Gaelic, although he declined to produce the original manuscripts. This set (arr. by Gavin Greig) comes from the *Harp and Claymore Collection*.

KEY:— F♯ MINOR
RELATIVE MAJOR:— A

a) The turn on the final quaver of bar 8 is placed above the note. It is in the form of a quintuplet (five notes played in the time of four of the same kind) and consists of the principal note, the note above, the principal note, the note (a semitone) below and the principal note:

Ex. 42

written   played

b) The term *cadenza* in bar 11 implies an improvisatory style of playing: beginning slowly, getting faster and then broadening out the tempo (rallentando) towards the end.

c) The sign *'tr'* (concluding bar) indicates a form of ornamentation known as the *trill*. Rarely used in Scottish fiddle-music, this consists of a rapid alternation of the principal note with the note a tone or, as in this case, a semitone above. As in this example, a turn is frequently inserted at the end of the trill:

Ex. 43

written   played

d) Use of the 4th position in this concluding bar, will not only simplify the fingering for the trill, but give a rich G-string sonority quite in keeping with the character of this piece.

The Lodge of Glen-Tana

Strathspey   J. Scott Skinner

With character

This first appeared in the *Elgin Collection* and subsequently in the *Logie Collection* where it is entitled simply *Glentana*. In the *Flowers of Scottish Melody* it is styled as being "after Charles Hardie's set", and it is the F♯-minor conclusion to this set which is employed here in preference to Skinner's original A-major.

Major and Minor

Reel

J. Murdoch Henderson

This tune from the *Flowers of Scottish Melody* is dedicated to Haydn P. Halstead, an Aberdeen musician whose critical advice Henderson enlisted while compiling that collection. The minor — relative major inflections in this tune make it the perfect reel to follow *Glen-Tana*.

The bracketed introductory E is played only on repeating the tune.

106

CHAPTER TWELVE

Multiple Stopping

Earl Haig (The Laird o' Bemersyde)

Pastoral

J. Scott Skinner

Slow and with dignity ♩ = c. 63

Field Marshal Earl Haig (1861 - 1928) was Commander-in-Chief of the British forces during the First World War. This tune, originally entitled *The Chief o' Bemersyde (A War Sermon)*, must have pleased Skinner, for, with characteristic modesty, he added at the foot of the manuscript, "a great effort I think".

This set is based on the version from J. Murdoch Henderson's *Scottish Music Maker* (1957).

Sixths, whether broken (bars 7 - 8) or double stopped (bars 9 - 12), are a prominent feature of this pastoral. Minor-6ths, indicated by an asterisk, are played with the fingers close together; major-6ths with the fingers a tone apart:—

Ex. 44

Matthew Hardie

Bill Hardie

Pastoral

With expression ♩ = 48-50

For some reason, no known musical tribute has previously been accorded to "The Scottish Stradivari". Bill Hardie rectified the omission with this expressive *Pastoral*. Certain names have special significance in any family, so it is perhaps little wonder that the composer's grandson now bears the name of his famous ancestor, Matthew Hardie.

The playing of double-stopped *thirds* will be greatly facilitated by keeping the 1st and 3rd fingers down as much as possible. The asterisked notes in Ex. 45 illustrate the different fingering-possibilities for ascending and descending:

Ex. 45

Tullochgorum

Strathspey
Boldly

D.S.

Tulach gorm is Gaelic for "the blue-green hill". J. Murdoch Henderson describes this tune as the *pons asinorum* of the strathspey-player, and certainly two of the greatest, Gow and Skinner, built their reputations on the performance of it. Scottish poets have been fully aware of its hypnotic power:— Burns called it "the first of songs", and poems in its praise were penned by the Rev. John Skinner (1721 - 1807) and Robert Fergusson (1750 - 1774) from whose "Daft Days" the following quotation comes:—

> Fiddlers! your pins in temper fix
> And roset weel your fiddlesticks;
> But banish vile Italian tricks
>   Frae out your quorum;
> Nor fortes wi' pianos mix —
>   Gie's Tullochgorum.

The tune first appeared in the second part of Robert Bremner's 1757 Collection.

It will be noted that this strathspey does not end with an incomplete bar to compensate for the opening quaver anacrusis. (The same applies to *Buckingham House*.) One can say only that these majestically primitive tunes somehow defy the conventions of neat metrical parcelling.

True intonation in *fifths* depends not only on the player (lateral movements of the finger can have a considerable effect), but also on the matching of the strings as to brand, material and quality. Do not mix brands or types of string, *i.e.*, stick to either metal or covered gut.

Practise Ex. 46 as broken chords and double stops:—

Ex. 46

The Devil and the Dirk

Reel   J. Scott Skinner

This reel comes from J. Scott Skinner's *The Scottish Violinist*. A much more elaborate set of this tune, the work of Gavin Greig, can be found in the *Harp and Claymore Collection*.

a) *Broken-octaves* feature in the second measure of this reel. Ex. 47 includes indications for keeping fingers down (very important in the performance of octaves) and position changing:

Ex. 47

b) Bars 5 - 8 are played throughout in 3rd-position.

Back to the Hills

* To Tom Fraser

(*This dedication appears in *The Scottish Violinist*.)

VAR. II

This impressive solo piece, also from *The Scottish Violinist*, demonstrates Skinner's treatment of variation as a vehicle for technical display.

    a)   The *double-stopped* octaves in bars 5 and 7 - 8 are so rare in Scottish fiddle-music as to make this piece almost unique. Practise Ex. 48, the scale of D harmonic minor, i) in broken octaves, as in Ex. 47, and ii) as written.

Ex. 48

    b)   *Quadruple-stopping*, a term describing chords composed of four notes, is a feature of bars 7, 18 and 22.

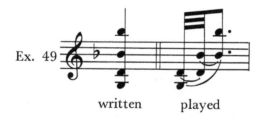

Ex. 49

written   played

    c)   *Triple-stopping* (see note to *The Banks of Spey*) occurs in bars 7, 17, 19 and 21.

    d)   The A-major *arpeggio* in bars 12 and 20 is fingered on a similar principle to the E-major *arpeggio* in *Mar Castle*. The present example is easier however in that the top two notes are playable in 7th position on the E string without the need for extensions or harmonics:

Ex. 50

I   IV   VII

Deoch Slainnte do'n airmailt tha Flannriose sa Ceannas
(Round with a health to Glorious Wellington)

Military Troop Air ♩.= 64

Simon Fraser
As played by A.J.H.

This is one of comparatively few original compositions which Fraser included in his "Knockie" Collection. Conceived originally as a patriotic song to commemorate the anniversary of the Battle of Waterloo, Fraser restyled it for the fiddle, being of the opinion that it made "a grand military troop when performed a little quicker".

The modern form of the above Gaelic title would be *Deoch Slàinte do'n armailt tha 'm Flànras, 's a Cheannas* which could be literally translated, "A health to the army in Flanders and its commander(s)".

   a) The high-C in bars 9 and 17 is played in 1st position with a semitone upward-extension of the 4th finger.
   b) When repeating the last measure, it gives the right air of finality if, in the fifth bar from the end, a pause is placed on the crotchet C.

Sir William Wallace

This fine patriotic pastoral from the *Harp and Claymore Collection* commemorates one of Scotland's bravest sons, Sir William Wallace (born c. 1270), who led the Scots to victory at Stirling in the uprising of 1297. The success was short-lived however, for Edward I defeated the Scottish forces the following year at the Battle of Falkirk. Wallace, captured and put on trial in London, was eventually executed at Smithfield in 1306.

Broaden out the last two beats before the reprise, beginning the melody again *a tempo*.

CHAPTER THIRTEEN

Drones and Other Bagpipe Influences

Macpherson's Lament

Lament, Traditional melody
Defiantly ♩ = 44-46

By Himself, 1700
As played by A.J.H.

The criminal exploits of James Macpherson (born c. 1675) ended in his being sentenced to the gallows in Banff, around 1700. The powers that be, aware that a reprieve was on the way, secured his execution by moving the town clock forward one hour.

Alternatively known as *Macpherson's Farewell* or *The Freebooter*, this tune was supposedly composed on the eve of the execution. As a last defiant gesture, Macpherson played the tune and then smashed the fiddle over his knee before going to the gallows.

This set is based on that of J. Scott Skinner's as found in *The Scottish Violinist*.

a) The bagpipe, not surprisingly, has had an influence on the style of much fiddle-music and on the technique of writing for the instrument itself. One of the most obvious results of this is in *drone-playing*, the performance of a melody on one string with the adjacent open string providing a primitive accompaniment. Care must be taken not to let the resonant open strings drown the melodic line. This problem can be avoided by angling the bow in favour of the stopped string.

b) In order to accommodate the drone G in bar 13, go up to 5th position on the final quaver of bar 12. Resume 1st position at the beginning of bar 14.

115

Buckingham House
(Athole Brose)

Strathspey tempo
With spirit

As played by J. Scott Skinner

VAR.

There is a certain doubt as to whether this tune was composed by Robert Mackintosh (c1745 - 1807) alias "Red Rob" or by his son Abraham Mackintosh (1769 - c1807). It is certainly credited to Abraham in Robert Mackintosh's 3rd Collection, (1796), a view supported in the *Harp and Claymore Collection* and *The Scottish Violinist* from which this set was taken. However, the *Glen Collection of Scottish Dance Music* (1891) declares "In 1796 he (Red Rob) set the music to a song called *Athol Brose*", and this concurs with the attribution in the *Logie Collection*.

Athole Brose is in fact a Scottish liqueur made from a mixture of honey and whisky. Niel Gow's associations with the beverage, are nicely captured in the following lines taken from Alexander Whitelaw's *Book of Scottish Song* (1844):

> You've surely heard o' the famous Niel, The man that played the fiddle weel;
> I wat he was a canty chiel, And dearly loved the whisky, O.
> And aye sin' he wore tartan hose, He dearly lo'ed the Athole Brose;
> And wae was he, you may suppose, To bid 'farewell to whisky', O.

To accommodate the high-C, begin the second and fourth measures in 2nd position, returning to 1st position on the semiquaver G♯ (bars 7 and 15).

116

Donald MacLean's Farewell to Oban

Archibald MacNeill
As played by Angus Grant

Pipe March ♩ = 70

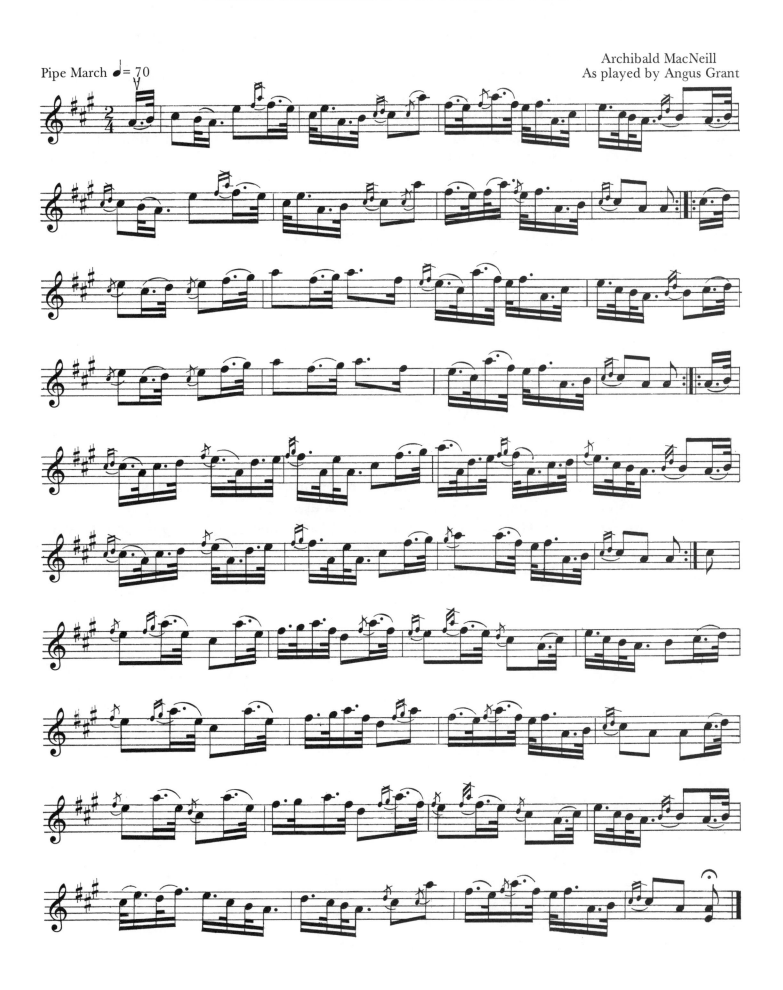

Angus Grant of Fort William is the most celebrated exponent of Highland West-coast fiddle-style. A left-handed fiddler, he began playing when he was thirteen and has gone on to win the fiddle-section in the Gaelic Mod on four occasions. More recently Angus took part in the American bi-centennial celebrations and he has toured extensively in Europe and Scandinavia.

Highland West-coast fiddle-style dates back to before the 1715 Jacobite Rebellion. With the ban on the bagpipes after the '45, many pipers turned their talents to the fiddle, contributing their own poetic, richly ornamented music to the fiddling tradition.

The work of Archibald MacNeill, the blind piper from the island of Gigha, this pipe march (and it is typical of the genre) consists of four strains, and relies heavily on variation technique. If the strathspey is the corner-stone of the East-coast fiddler's repertoire, then the pipe-march holds a comparable position in the music of the West highlands.

a) The ornamentation employed here aims to recreate the spirit rather than the letter of pipe style. Embellishments are written in the manner of the acciaccatura, i.e., with a diagonal stroke through their stems ♪♪ ♪♪♪ , and should be played in a similar "crushed-in" style.

b) The ornament consisting of the principal note and the note a minor third above (as on the second beat of bar 1) is highly characteristic of this style.

Ex. 51

c) The treatment of the *acciaccatura* is unusual, often proceeding to the principal note by a leap, as in bar 2, or from the note a tone above, as in bar 7.

d) A feature of Angus Grant's style — observable in performances of this and the following ⁶₈ pipe march — is a tendency to play the note G♯ (2nd finger on the E string) more natural than sharp. This trait is obviously attributable to the influence of the "pipe-mode" (see page 51).

Lady Dorothea Stewart Murray's Wedding March

Aeneas Rose
As played by Angus Grant

Pipe March ♩.= 92

Born in Kingussie, Aeneas Rose (1832 - 1905) was pipe major of the Atholl Highlanders for some forty years. This march, composed in 1895, and the following Retreat Air are taken from Volume I of the *Scots Guards — Standard Settings of Pipe Music* (1954). Like the preceding $\frac{2}{4}$ Pipe-march, they are examples of *Ceol Beag* ("Small" or "little" music), i.e., the lighter side of the bagpipe repertoire applicable to dancing and marching.

According to Angus Grant, "In $\frac{6}{8}$ pipe-marches highland-fiddlers use mostly the middle of the bow".

Far O'er Struy

J. P. MacLeod
As played by Angus Grant

Retreat Air ♩ = 94

A piper and pipe-maker, John Peter MacLeod of Tain achieved the distinction of winning the gold medal for pibroch at Inverness in 1907. This is an example of a "Retreat" air, a form popular with West-coast fiddlers. The late "Pibroch" Alex Mackenzie was a master at playing them and this tune was a particular favourite of his.

The "Struy" is a high winding hill-road above the Dornoch Firth.

a) As illustrated here the playing of octaves and fifths (redolent of the bagpipe drones) is a common feature of West-coast style.
b) In order to bring out the *cantabile* quality this tune should be bowed with fairly long strokes.

CHAPTER FOURTEEN

Scordatura

Kilrack's Strathspey

Strathspey

Boldly accented

This strathspey comes from Niel Gow's *First Collection of Strathspey Reels*. All the tunes in this section employ *scordatura* (mis-tuning), a device whereby abnormal string tunings are employed for special effects. This technique dates from the days of the lute and the viol where the particular tuning to be adopted was indicated at the beginning of the tune — a practice which has also been employed in Scottish fiddling.

The tuning here involves sharpening the G-string a tone to A and similarly the D-string to E. Consequently all the notes on the re-tuned strings are raised by a tone. It is nevertheless customary to notate the music as if the tuning were normal, with the lower notes sounding a tone higher than written:

Ex. 52

written

sounds

The (editorial) addition to the first key-signature in each case acts as a reminder that the lower two strings are to be fingered as if the piece were in G major.

121

Of this particular tuning (A-E-a-e), Grove's *Dictionary of Music and Musicians* (1927 Edition) says, "it is extremely favourable to simplicity of fingering in the key of A". (The A-E fifth in bar 1 can be played on open strings instead of double-stopped.) "It is frequently employed by Scottish reel players and in their hands has a singularly rousing effect".

Greig's Pipes

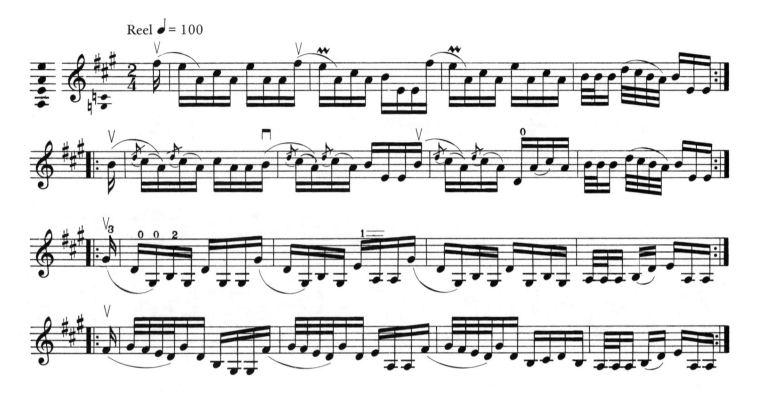

The A-E-a-e tuning, again employed here, gives the fiddle something of the resonant, strident quality of the bagpipes, a fact reflected in the title of this fine reel. The above set is based on two previously published sets in Joshua Campbell's *Newest and Best Reels* (c. 1778) and the Gows' *Complete Repository* (Part I, 1799).

Tunes such as this are often played at the end of an evening's music-making, for the obvious reason that only one re-tuning of the instrument is necessitated. The practical considerations of *scordatura*-playing might persuade the owners of good instruments to use a less cherished fiddle — especially when the re-tuning involves a raising of the pitch.

Da Auld Foula Reel

Slowish Reel ♩ = 96

As played by Tom Anderson

This Shetland reel was the traditional accompaniment for a special dance from the Island of Foula. On the Island of Yell it was known as *Da Auld Reel*.

Scordatura is a feature closely associated with the Norwegian Hardanger fiddle. Indeed Shetland music generally has closer affinities with Scandinavia than with the Scottish-mainland tradition.

CHAPTER FIFTEEN

Staccato Bowings and other 'Italian Tricks'

Balmoral Castle

March

Bold and bright

J. Scott Skinner

Queen Victoria, having eventually heard of Skinner's not inconsiderable abilities as a dancing master, commanded him to include the tenantry of Balmoral Castle (her summer residence) among his pupils. This two-variation set of the tune comes from the *Harp and Claymore Collection*.

The detached quavers in bars 1, 2, 3 and 11 are executed with *martelé* bowing (notated with staccato dots and accents). As the term implies, this is a detached, hammered style of bowing and is best executed in the upper third of the bow. A rotary forearm-pressure is applied to the bow during the pause between each note, the pressure being relaxed as the bow moves. Begin Ex. 53 on an up bow:

Ex. 53

King Robert the Bruce

Patriotic March
Boldly

J. Scott Skinner

VAR.

A worthy companion piece to the same composer's *Sir William Wallace*. Appropriately, the year that Wallace was executed (1306), Robert the Bruce (1274 - 1329) led a second Scottish rebellion. This culminated in the triumphant Battle of Bannockburn in 1314, after which Bruce was crowned king of an independent Scotland.

a) Taken from the *Harp and Claymore Collection* this march requires the use of *up-bow staccato* notated with staccato dots and a smooth or extended straight slur.

This stroke consists of a series of detached notes produced in the one (up) bow, and is best executed from the point to the middle. The rotary movement of the forearm, referred to in the study of the *martelé*, again comes into play in articulating each note. The staccato may gain from a certain stiffening of the forearm.

Ex. 54

b) Detached quavers are, generally, played martelé. A more legato treatment of bars 9 - 10 will however provide an effective contrast.

Madam Neruda

J. Scott Skinner

Hornpipe

As played by A.J.H.

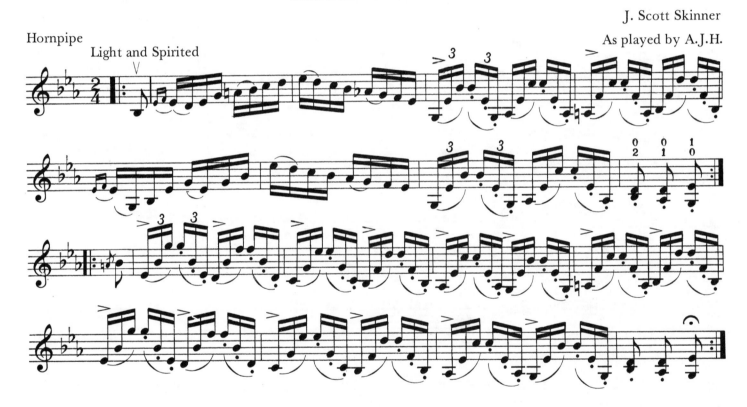

Wilhelmina Neruda (1839 - 1911) was one of the most distinguished concert violinists of her generation. She is perhaps better known under her married name of Lady Hallé, her husband being Sir Charles Hallé, founder of the famous English orchestra.

a) Skinner described this hornpipe from the *Logie Collection* as an "arpeggio movement in E♭", the arpeggios being taken with a leaping staccato stroke known as *saltando* bowing (notated with staccato dots on every second group of three notes and smooth slurs).

Practise Ex. 55 (i) in the middle of the bow, maintaining just enough pressure on the stick to prevent the bow from springing; (ii) relaxing the pressure gradually and allowing the bow to spring through the natural resilience of the stick. An accent on the first note of each group of six will help give the necessary momentum:

Ex. 55

b) Chordal, triple-stopped practice of bars 9 - 15 will increase left-hand facility. Practise Ex. 56 (i) with successive down bows; (ii) with alternating down and up bows.

Ex. 56

Banks

Classical Hornpipe

Parazotti
As played by J. Scott Skinner

Parazotti was the grandson of an immigrant Italian violinist who settled in Glasgow. In Köhlers' *Violin Repository Bk. I* this tune appears under the title *Mrs. Taff.* The lady in question resided on the West coast of Scotland and it was under her roof that Parazotti composed this *descriptive hornpipe*. It was inspired by the sights and sounds of a river in spate — the arpeggios representing the surging water and the cadential up-bow staccati the noise of the stones being carried down by the deluge. The alternative title, *Banks*, is simply a shortened version of Parazotti's original *Banks of The River*. (I am indebted to Tom Anderson for this information.)

This masterly hornpipe, which appears in *The Harp and Claymore Collection* in a splendid arrangement by Gavin Greig, is traditionally preceded by the slow strathspey *The Dean Brig o' Edinburgh*.

a) As well as employing up-bow staccato and saltando bowing, the opening of *Banks* employs *ricochet* or *thrown-bow*, notated with staccato dots and smooth slurs. The bow is dropped onto the string from the height of approximately half an inch and allowed to bounce for as many times as there are notes.

The up-bow variety, used here, is performed in the upper half of the bow:

b) The two concluding quavers in bars 4 and 12, and the opening of the second measure or section make a feature of repeated down-bow recovery. Play these passages with the lower half of the bow.

The Peterhead Polka

William Stephen
As played by Bill Hardie

Polka

With style and elegance ♩ = 76

D.C. al Fine

William Stephen, a native of the Aberdeenshire town of Peterhead, originally published this fine polka in a version for piano solo.

Sautillé bowing, notated with staccato dots, is a feature here in bars 17 to 18 and 21 to 26. Also known as "bouncing", "dancing", "feather" or "springing" bow, this stroke should be executed in the middle of the bow.

Practise Ex. 58—

a) With a very small detaché in the middle of the bow, maintaining just enough pressure to prevent the bow from springing, and

b) relaxing the pressure gradually, and allowing the bow to spring through the natural resilience of the stick.

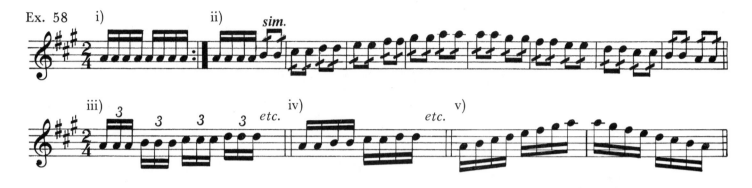

Madame Vanoni

This unusual hornpipe comes from the *Harp and Claymore Collection*.

a) *Artificial harmonics* are a feature of this tune (bars 5, 6 and 15). These are produced by stopping the 1st finger firmly on the string and by touching lightly with the 4th finger a perfect 4th above. The resultant note sounds two octaves above the stopped note. In

Ex. 59 the lowest note indicates the stopping finger, the diamond the placing of the 4th and the upper note the pitch- and time-value.

Position-changes are indicated in Roman numerals and the notes marked with an asterisk are natural harmonics played with the 3rd finger lightly touching the string.

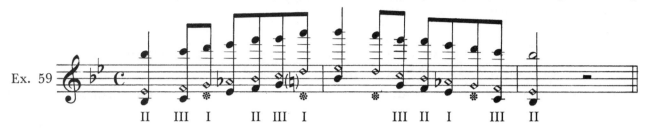

Le Messe

Violin Solo

Polka tempo

J. Scott Skinner

132

Trio

VAR.

The title of this tune refers to a famous Stradivarius violin made in 1716: "the finest violin in the world", as a footnote to the tune in the *Harp and Claymore* would have us believe. At that time (1904) it was owned by a Mr. Crawford of Trinity, Leith, who had purchased the instrument for the sum of £2000.

If many of these concluding pieces have more in common with the 19th century school of violin virtuosity than with the world of fiddle-music, then it is a reminder that the repertoire of the youthful Skinner was very much a mixed-bag of stock classical showpieces and fiddle music. The appendix to the *Miller o' Hirn Collection* quotes a programme given in Peterhead on April 9th, 1879. Skinner's contribution to the first half included:

> Overture "Figaro" . . . . Mozart
>
> Violin solo "O a' the Airts" . . . . Marshall
>
> Scottish selection — "Auld Robin Gray"
>
> "Mrs Scott Skinner", Strathspey
>
> "Miller o' Hirn" and "Auld Wheel" . . . . Scott Skinner
>
> Violin solo — Seventh air in E major . . . . De Bériot
>
> Violin solo — Air Varie op 10 . . . . P. Rode
>
> Rondo "Pizzicato" . . . . Paganini

Le Messe introduces the technique of *left-hand pizzicato*. As the name implies, both the *pizzicato* (plucking the string with the finger) and the *fingering* are executed by the left hand. The notation used is that of a cross (+).

a) The device is presented at its simplest using open strings (as in bars 1 and 3) and is executed by the 4th finger. The introductory demi-semiquaver passage is produced by an exaggerated finger-articulation.

b) In bars 25 - 26 and 29 - 30 (Trio section) the stopped notes are executed with the 1st finger and plucked with the 4th. This necessitates the following position changes:

c) In the Variation (bars 33, 35 and 37) Skinner multiplies the difficulties by making simultaneous use of right- and left-hand pizzicato. Take the top notes L.H. pizzicato and pluck the lower notes with the index finger of the right hand.

   Alternatively the *Harp and Claymore* set directs that the lower notes may be played *arco* (with the bow).

The President

VAR. I

Trio

VAR. II

Trio

137

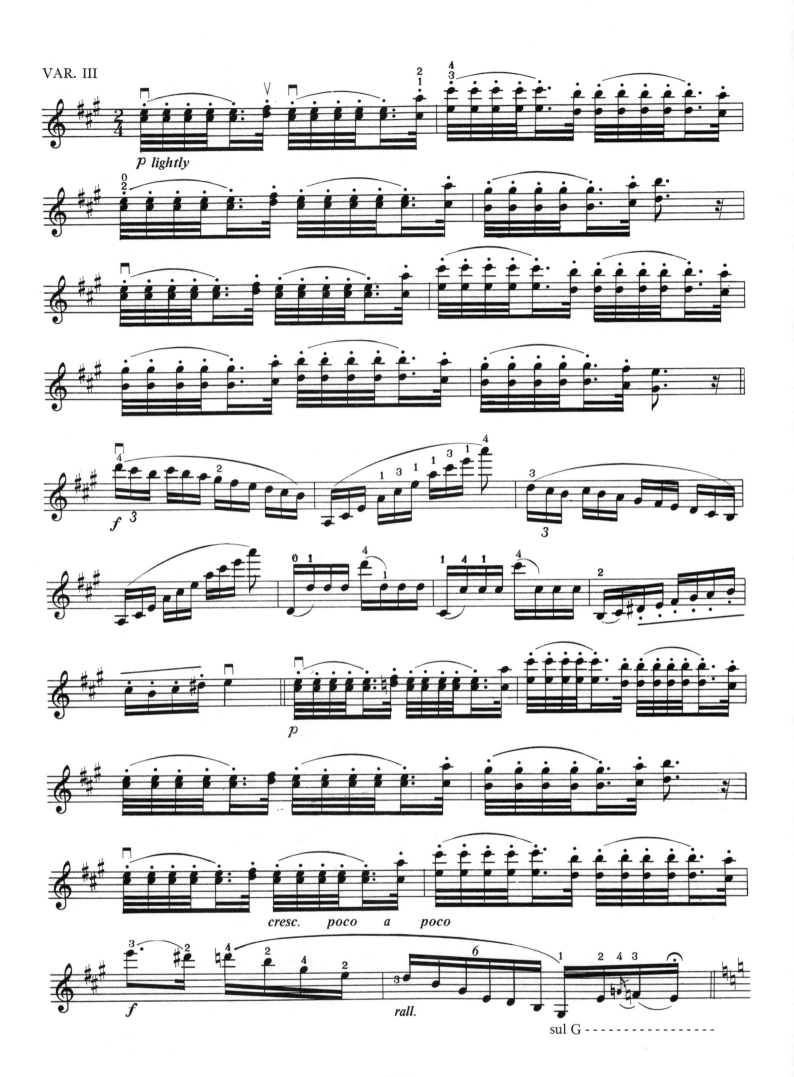

The title of this celebrated war-horse reminds one that Skinner made two trips to the United States of America, in 1893 and 1926. The second visit, undertaken at the age of 82, was to take part in a World fiddling-championship in Lewiston, Portland Bay, in the State of Maine.

Most fiddlers have a love-hate relationship with this "violin solo with variations", taken from *The Scottish Violinist*, and can often be found practising its not inconsiderable difficulties well out of earshot of any potential rivals.

a) Because of the D♯ and G♯ in the turn, the opening trills should be fingered in half-position, continuing in this position for the following two notes. The fingering pattern for the remainder of these arpeggios has already been explained. (For bars 1 and 3 see *Mar Castle* and bar 2 see *Back to the Hills*.)

b) Using natural harmonics, bars 13 and 15 (polka theme) can be played in 3rd position. The diamond-shaped notes indicate the placing of the finger:—

Ex. 61

c) Variation I introduces the use of *spiccato* bowing, notated with staccato dots. This stroke is best executed near the centre of gravity of the bow, i.e., its balancing point. Generated by the arm, the bowing movement forms an arc, coming in contact with the string and glancing off again. *Spiccato* might be loosely thought of as a slowed-down *sautillé* (see *Peterhead Polka*) and indeed the same exercises and procedure can be adopted, but, of course, at a slower tempo (approximately ♩ = 80). A *detaché* treatment of the middle-8 bars of Variation I will contrast effectively with the *spiccato*.

d) Variation III and the Finale employ ricochet-bowing. It is used here in its down-bow form and performed in the middle of the bow:—

Ex. 62

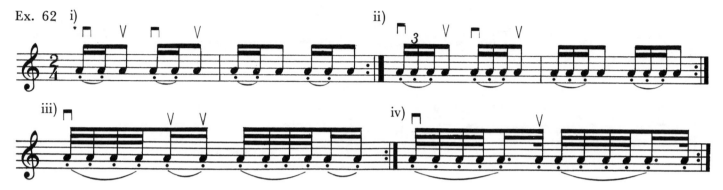

e) The concluding two bars of the Adagio (page 139) employ alternative fingerings; the choice is between a conventional move from 3rd to 1st position (the fingering is given in brackets) or the continuous use of the 4th position. Although more challenging, the latter fingering is recommended as the passage concerned can then, for the most part, be played on the 3rd (D) string.

For nought can cheer the heart sae weel,
As can a canty Highland reel;
It even vivifies the heel
          To skip and dance:
Lifeless is he wha canna feel
          Its influence.

From *The Daft Days*
Robert Fergusson (1750 - 74)

GLOSSARY

A'	all; one
Airts	directions
Amang	among
An'	and
Anither	another
Auld	old
Birly	briskly, quickly
Brent-new	brand new
Brig	a bridge
Canna	cannot
Canty	pleasant, cheerful
Cauld	cold
Chiel	fellow
Da	the (Shetland)
Daft days	holidays at Christmas and New Year
Deil	devil
Dirk	dagger
Dirl	sound
Doon	down
Dram	a glass of whisky
E'e	eye
Frae	from
Fu'	full
Ghillie	a youth (Gaelic); man servant
Gie's	give us
Gin	if
Haand	hand (Shetland)
Ha'e	have
Haund	a hand
Ilka	every
Ither	other
Kirk	church
Langer	longer
Lave	remainder, rest
Lo'ed	loved
Loon	lad

Mair	more
'Mang	among
Mony	many
Nae	not; no
Neuk	corner
Nought	nothing
O'	of
O'er	over
O't	of it
Pins	fiddle-pegs
Pocky	pocket, purse
Ranting	high spirited, roistering
Reamin-fu'	full to overflowing
Red-wud	headstrong, mad
Roset	to resin the bow hair
Sae	so
Saut	salt
Sean triubhas	old trousers (Gaelic)
Shakins	remains
Sin'	since
Sma'	small
Stile	style
Tae	to
Th'	the
Thocht	thought
Trews	trousers
Wae	sad
Wat	know
Wee	little, young
Weel	well
Weel-gaun	smooth-working
Wha	who
Wha'll	who will
Wheelie	a wheel
Wi'	with
Ye	you